Leave No Child Inside

A Selection of Essays from Orion *Magazine*

ORION

Orion Readers are published by *Orion* magazine.
All essays appeared in *Orion*.

Orion
187 Main Street, Great Barrington, Massachusetts 01230
Telephone: 888/909-6568
Fax: 413/528-0676
www.orionmagazine.org

After its appearance in *Orion Afield,* Robert Michael Pyle's essay "Naming Names" was published in the book *The Tangled Bank: Writings from* Orion; it is reprinted here with permission of Oregon State University Press.

Design by Hans Teensma/Impress

Cover photograph by Steven David Johnson,
www.stevendavidjohnson.com

ISBN: 978-1-935713-08-1

Dedicated to Christopher Nye

CONTENTS

FOREWORD

THIS IS A BOOK about education for connection with the earth—about direct, unhurried engagement with nature as a portal for the full unfolding of the physical, intellectual, emotional, moral, and spiritual capabilities of our human nature. It is about education for ecological citizenship, because from knowing and loving particular places, people draw motivation to protect the integrity of those places. Collectively, these authors are asking a question: if we were to create communities and schools that educate children and youth to love the earth, know their place in the web of life, and act responsibly, what would they look like? Hearteningly, they suggest many exemplary answers.

The essays gathered in *Leave No Child Inside* address education at every level, from birth to adulthood, in and out of schools. From the time of his son's birth, observes Medicine Grizzlybear Lake, his son was bonded to his parents, the Great Spirit, Mother Earth, Grandfather Sun, and Grandmother Moon in traditional ceremonies. For early and middle childhood, David Sobel advocates environmental education that allows children to engage with nature on their own active terms, building forts, climbing trees, wading in creeks, catching frogs, and making mud pies. He summarizes research that indicates that this kind of full-bodied encounter with nature characterizes the childhoods of people who take action for the environment later in life. Belle Boggs and Elise Rymer describe public school programs that teach students science, literacy, and the humanities through activities like growing gardens, studying local plants and animals, tracing the natural and cultural history of their watershed, and investigating environmental issues that grip their communities.

This type of place-based education involves learning the cultural and political history of a place as well as its natural history. It is consistent with Thomas Jefferson's ideal of an educated citizenry who know their local places well, creating a foundation for responsible self-governance. Eric Reece and John Elder show how an education of this kind can be extended to college and university programs. Brenda Peterson describes how teenagers can tap their power and critical agency through identification with animals in particular, and Robert Michael Pyle defends the identification of animals and plants as a means for all ages to know "fellowship in the neighborhood of living things."

One of the barriers to connecting with nature, however, is our society's infatuation with digital representations of the world. Stephen Talbott and Lowell Monke sensitively untangle the moral and political choices that are at stake here. While neither author is against the use of digital technologies at appropriate times for appropriate purposes, they argue the necessity of first learning empathy and moral responsibility through direct encounters with the world, with its richer possibilities and real limits.

Richard Louv, whose book *Last Child in the Woods* inspired the movement to "Leave No Child Inside," puts education in its broadest context—guided by the advice of Martin Luther King Jr., who said that the success of any social movement depends on its ability to show a world where people will want to go. Connecting children with nature is, Louv argues, a "gateway" issue that can unite people of many professions and political persuasions around a vision of communities where nature is woven into the fabric of everyday life, in neighborhoods as well as schools, for the health and happiness of children and people of all ages.

Taken together, the essays in this book paint hopeful and convincing pictures of a world where people will want to go, and to which children can contribute through the actions that they inspire in adults and through their own untamed creative agency.

LOUISE CHAWLA
Professor in the Environmental Design Program
at the University of Colorado, Boulder

Leave
No Child
Inside

STEPHEN L. TALBOTT

WHY IS THE MOON GETTING FARTHER AWAY?

IF YOU'VE EVER LOOKED through the wrong end of a telescope, you know that this instrument has opposite effects, depending on how you use it. What may be less obvious is that even normal use of the telescope can be rather paradoxical.

Who does not marvel at the incomprehensibly remote galaxies brought near to us by the modern telescope? Our lives would be sadly impoverished without these images. And yet, by expanding the universe without limit, isolating our vision from our other senses and encouraging us to view ourselves as chance objects among billions and billions of objects, far from the center of things, this same telescope has whispered to many: "You are an accident, lost in a vast, wind-blown desert where the grains of sand are stars."

Things, apparently, can be brought closer while at the same time becoming more remote, more disconnected from us. "We had to travel to the moon in 1969," surmises psychologist Robert Romanyshyn, not because it had come so near to us, but "because it had gone so far away."

Did we, like the middle-aged man seeking the long-lost love of his youth, travel to the moon in order to see whether, in our state of alienation, we still had a connection to it? Did we vaguely hope that the magic, the dying coals of an earlier flame, might be rekindled through this reunion? If so, the question is whether our chosen instruments of approach were self-defeating. If the telescope not only brings things nearer, but also transforms and objectifies space in a way that can easily make us feel like chance intruders, it is not at all clear, for example, that the rockets within which we fling our bodies through this alien space are vehicles of reconciliation and homecoming.

Home, of course, is where every child belongs. But a world that feels like home is increasingly what we deny our children—this despite the televisions and internet connections that bring the world into the intimacy of their bedrooms. Such devices only accentuate the central educational challenge of our day: how do we help the child find his own connections to the world?

The Loss of Significance

I don't think modern technology *necessarily* alienates us from the world it mediates. But a lot depends on our recognizing how it *can* do so. And the first thing to say here is that the problem is not and never was one of scale. It is badly mistaken to think: "The telescope reveals the earth as a mere flyspeck in the cosmic infinitudes, so of course we can no longer consider ourselves significant in the old religious sense." That's as confused a bit of thinking as any nonsense for which we ridicule the ancients. As C. S. Lewis reminded us, "Ptolemy knew just as well as Eddington that the earth was infinitesimal in comparison with the whole content of space." Nor,

Lewis adds, do we really believe that a six-foot man is more important than a five-foot man, or that a tree is more important than a human, or a leg more important than a brain.

Spatial dimension has never been a measure of significance. When we argue today that big is significant and small is insignificant, we merely testify to our loss of any sense for what is significant. Size, after all, is a matter of quantity, but significance is qualitative.

So if telescopes and other instruments of modern science express our alienation from the world, it is not because of the dimensional scales they introduce, but because we have tended, with their encouragement, to substitute dimension for the things that count. Employing such tools, we are invited to ignore our own significant connections to the world, which are never merely quantitative.

But it is not only the moon and planets and stars that have come to seem remote from us. The historical psychologist J. H. van den Berg has traced the alienation of Westerners from their own physical landscape. He offers a fascinating survey of the past several centuries, and after characterizing the nature-ecstasy of the Romantics, he considers the altered experience of our own day:

> Many of the people who, on their traditional trip to the Alps, ecstatically gaze at the snow on the mountain tops and at the azure of the transparent distance, do so out of a sense of duty. They . . . are simulating an emotion which they do not actually feel. It is simply not permissible to sigh at the vision of the great views and to wonder, for everyone to hear, whether it was really worth the trouble. And yet the question would be fully justified; all one has to do is see the sweating and sun burned crowd, after it has streamed out of the train or the bus, plunge with resignation into the recommended

beauty of the landscape to know that for a great many the trouble is greater than the enjoyment. (The Changing Nature of Man)

Harsh as this may seem, I suspect that most of us would have to admit to our own experience of the tour bus syndrome. It's as if we knew somewhere within us that we *ought* to feel a powerful response to the wonders of nature. And we do feel something—but it is all too often vague. Somehow the threads connecting us to our surroundings have grown so tenuous that we find ourselves facing a forlorn blank. We *want* the powerful experience—we may even feel guilty for not having it—but it's not there.

So what do we do? We "capture" the experience on film. "I've seen people in the Everglades come onto the walkway with their video equipment, take a picture, and go away," says Massachusetts naturalist John Hanson Mitchell.

We take much the same approach toward births, graduations, marriages, and the like. It's as if, not trusting our vague, subjective experience of the event, we need to freeze and objectify it in the hope that we can come up with a more fitting appreciation later. Of course, what the stored image will enable us to recall and appreciate most vividly is the experience of picture-taking.

Living in a Virtual World

There are many other symptoms of our estrangement from the world. I once spoke to an extremely intelligent high school graduate who was not sure in which direction the sun rose. Bill McKibben tells of a camping trip during which he learned that adolescents who had lived their whole lives in the Adirondacks did not know there was such a thing as the Milky Way. I've heard an astronomy teacher lament that, since *Star Wars*, students are not very interested in the "boring" view through a telescope, and a naturalist complain about the television generation's disinterest in the not-sufficiently-exotic local flora and fauna.

None of this reflects a shortage of information. The problem is that today something is substituting for the child's intimacy with the world. And if you want to know the nature of the substitution, consider the lenses, video screens, instrument panels, windows, phones, loudspeakers, books, faxes, billboards, newspapers, magazines, and various protected environments through which we gauge our relations to the world. How can the child possibly feel that the natural world counts for anything at all?

Michael Crichton tells of a young boy who looked at all the sea creatures in a public aquarium and asked, "Is this virtual reality or real reality?" The audience, I think, was expected to be disconcerted by the boy's cluelessness. Rightly so. But let's look closely at the situation:

After a couple of hours watching Saturday morning cartoons, the boy is handed a lunch extracted from various cans, bags, and cartons and cooked in a microwave oven. Then he leaves the house with his parents and gets into the family station wagon. Driving off with the radio playing, they pass blindly through the local environment at fifty miles per hour, and then negotiate the traffic and lights of downtown, where virtually everything to be seen has been constructed. Eventually they park their car in a huge lot near a large, concrete building, enter the lobby of the building, buy tickets at a movie theater–like ticket window, walk through a large hall filled with weird, eye-catching promotional posters, go down some stairs, and then, along with a crowd of total strangers, they enter a series of rooms whose glass walls display the brightly colored forms of exotic fish dredged up from the bottom of the Atlantic.

Now, ask yourself: Is this boy peculiar for having some uncertainties about the "reality" he is being hustled through? Or are *we* the ones hopelessly out of touch, failing to appreciate the problems of disconnection and incoherence written all over the surface of our daily lives?

In my opinion, the most revealing thing about this story is our own surprise at the boy's puzzlement. The degree to which we have subjected him to a manufactured, chaotic, and disconnected sequence of images and experiences simply escapes our notice.

Now, I happen to believe that the construction of truly human environments is no bad thing. In fact, it is one of our highest callings. But there is no denying that what we have constructed so far is more an assault upon the world and a fragmentation of it than a crowning of it.

Realistically, I think we should have expected the boy to exclaim, "Wow! Where'd you get those awesome 3-D screensavers?" But whatever the child's response, we can be absolutely sure of one thing: his experience had almost nothing in common with that of the young Tom Brown, Jr., who was mucking about in a local stream, entertaining the crawdads, at the fateful moment when he met Stalking Wolf. That stream became a teaching resource for Stalking Wolf because it was connected via a thousand pathways to Tom's interests and daily existence. It was there.

Those of you who have read Tom Brown's books know that Stalking Wolf, the old Apache scout, had a peculiar way of teaching his young student during their ten-year partnership. Stalking Wolf was no citizen of the Age of Information, for his "coyote method" came close to being a flat-out refusal to divulge information. In response to questions he would say things such as "Go ask the mice," or "Feed the birds." The student would immediately be off on a new adventure of days' or weeks' duration.

To teach fire-making with a bow drill, Stalking Wolf gave Tom a piece of oak from which it would have been impossible to coax a live coal. Only much later (and after long struggle) did Tom discover that, using cedar wood, he could start a fire almost instantly, thanks to the techniques he had honed so well upon the recalcitrant oak. So now, not only did he know how to make a fire, but, much more importantly, his skills grew out of an understanding of the world in which he was imbedded.

Tom went on to develop survival and tracking abilities that seem all but supernatural to many observers. Then he devoted his life to teaching others.

Interestingly, though, he quickly gave up the coyote method of teaching. It simply doesn't work for most people today. They just get lost and discouraged because, unlike Tom with the crawdads, they have no time and they're not connected to anything. Or, rather, their connections are one-dimensional, abstract, arbitrary, and of uncertain reality. The creek is one thing, but how do you make a child's world out of a concrete building with exotic "screensavers"?

We *can* begin to attack the problem, but it involves grounding the child in a world to which he can relate on as many different levels as possible.

Learning the Language of Horses

The Man Who Listens to Horses is the remarkable story of how Monty Roberts, by observing horses—by listening to their language of movement and gesture—learned to relate to them as a friend and collaborator rather than as a tyrant. In hundreds of demonstrations Roberts has persuaded wild or untrained horses to submit to bridle, saddle, and rider without any use of constraining force. Employing his own body to speak the horse's language, Roberts plays out a subtle drama of horse behavior in which he must read and respond to the horse's "utterances," right down to the fear or intelligence or curiosity shining through its eyes. Finally he turns his back on the horse and walks away—whereupon this often high-strung animal slowly comes up to him from behind to await further collaboration. It often takes less than thirty minutes to saddle and mount a horse that has never been ridden before. (Roberts is the son of a more traditional horse trainer who used ropes, pain, and subjugation to "break" horses—a process typically lasting six weeks and not infrequently resulting in injury to the horse.)

Roberts has achieved similar "join-up" with deer, and he remarks that it is always a stirring moment for him when such an animal agrees to be touched by the human hand. But what is going on here? How can it be that Roberts is such an isolated case, and such an eccentric within his profession? If we can put a man on the moon, how can we be so blind in our understanding of the animals we have employed for millennia? Well, as I have suggested, we may have become blind in part because we have sent a man to moon—that is, because we have been interested only in the exploration and conquering of objects, and you cannot hold a conversation with an object.

I found the story a powerful testimonial to our culture's instinctive conviction that every problem can be solved by bringing the right combination of materials and forces to bear upon it. We are not taught to look for the nuances of meaning and gesture through which we can hold a delicate, yet powerful conversation with the problem. (Ask yourself, incidentally, whether it's easier or harder to find these nuances in computermediated communication.)

There are a few things I would like to say in relating Roberts's story to education. The first is that we've not lacked the opportunity to learn what Roberts learned. Many of the things he learned have in fact been learned before. Roberts's half-Indian uncle told him how the Cherokees used to capture wild horses: at the end of an extended conversation through movement, they would walk into a corral with the horses willingly following them. A book by John Solomon Rarey in the mid-1800s created a huge stir throughout Europe by detailing the dramatic potentials of collaboration between man and horse. In 1858 a writer in the *Illustrated London News* predicted that Rarey's name "will rank among the great social reformers of the nineteenth century." But instead the book—along with its insights—was forgotten.

Something in our culture works powerfully against a sensitive, participative understanding of the world, often obliterating that understanding wherever it does arise. I believe that a primary task of education today is to counter this one-sidedness.

Second, the "delicate conversation" I mentioned a moment ago is not a casual exchange of information. Roberts's understanding arose from close observation of the finest details, repeated again and again while he was wholly immersed in the horse's environment. He tried to experience that environment as the horse experienced it. This is not at all the sort of knowledge, or information, that can be passed automatically from one mind or database to another.

In our drive to achieve frontal, effective power over the world, we have generally not had the patience to cultivate the very different, but no less effective powers of intimacy and sympathy. But if we want to redress the imbalance of our culture, surely this is where we must apply ourselves.

Third, Roberts *loved* horses. He could not bear to see them suffer, and his desire to understand them was a passion that drove him through great danger. You do not hear much about love in the contemporary arguments for wired schools.

Fourth, if there is any one place where this intimacy and sympathy, this immersion in the concrete environment of the other, this delicate reading of nuance and meaning, is most required, it is in human relations. Here the task must surely be even more complex and challenging than it is with horses. Yet one can fairly say that the future hangs upon our capacity to read the other person in his own world—certainly much more than it hangs on our ability to pass information around. Where you find social breakdown, you will also find people who don't even know how to begin the process of mutual understanding that brought Monty Roberts and wild horses into fruitful engagement.

Once we recognize this, we can hardly avoid the uncomfortable sense that our society has gone quite out of its mind in making the computer the tool of choice for connecting people—and in particular for connecting young students—to "sources of information." The computer undeniably inserts a distance between people that must be overcome. As a result it is much easier for us to objectify others—to treat them in terms of our own needs. It disconnects words from the speaker, ignores much of our nonverbal communication, and occludes the larger environment that is always speaking and being spoken through us.

I am not saying that the limitations of the computer, any more than the limitations of the telescope, are insuperable. We can and must learn to overcome them. But they are hardly instruments for countering the prevailing imbalance of society. And if it is true that the twenty-first century will be the age of unimaginably sophisticated and pervasive technologies, then counterbalance is what we will need most.

A Chickadee Lesson

I would like to conclude with a much more humble, personal story. For some time I've been interested in birds, although I haven't been able to do much more than begin to observe and listen as best I can in my own neighborhood. But a couple of months ago, I decided to see whether I could coax a few birds into feeding from my hand.

I spent four days—about an hour and a half per day—sitting on the steps of my house, beside a bench, which happens to be just a few feet from a mix of trees, weeds, and brush that makes an ideal habitat for many birds. I spread seed around so as to encourage the birds to come closer and closer to me as I sat motionless.

On the fourth day the first black-capped chickadee, with a lightning-quick peck, stole a sunflower seed from my hand and fled for his life. Soon, however, he and some of his kin were jumping right into my hand, and eventually an occasional one would go about his precision business of punching open the seed while holding it against my thumb.

Chickadees, of course, don't really count, since they're half human already. But other birds—even including the storm troopers, which most people call blue jays—have gotten progressively curious. So far, juncos, titmice, and nuthatches have braved the human hand. And at times, amid a flurry of wings and sudden little air blasts against the face, I find my head, arms, legs, and feet all used as temporary perches.

Now, rest assured: I am no man who listens to birds. I have no special sympathies or skills—and in fact am probably deprived in this regard. I simply went rather mechanically through the steps required to accustom the birds to a human feeding station. After I had done this, my grown son took my place and had birds feeding from his hand on the first try. A child could do the same.

I am coming to appreciate the chickadee in ways I never would have thought possible. But the prolonged stillness and quiet of my vigils are themselves valuable. I see things I would never see while moving about normally. Once a hawk, attended by a highly upset blue jay, landed on a low branch about ten yards in front of my face, scattering all the smaller birds. A pileated woodpecker, I discovered to my surprise, sometimes visits our little grove. And I've watched a rabbit drowsing for an hour or so in the filtered sunlight just inside the brush line.

All this has been an epiphany for me. It's been all I can do to restrain myself from collaring everyone I meet and exclaiming, "I had a bird eating out of my hand today!"

But this, I suggest, is a sad state of affairs. Here I am, fifty-one years old, and I am dis covering for the first time what it can be like to "join up" with a little bit of nature. Others, of course, are not as slow and backward as I. But it seems to me there is a question that might occur to anyone who has had such an experience. What would it cost us to wire, say, every third-grade class to a few birds? Just chickadee feed.

And the same question, with the same answer, applies to countless other aspects of nature. Yet we are spending billions of dollars to give our children computer-mediated, distance-increasing experiences of the world.

Where are our priorities? Children are not at risk of missing out on the fact that we're becoming a wired society. We don't need help making sure that future generations embrace technology. Technophobia just doesn't happen to be the dominant trait of our society. What we need is *balance* and *connection*.

We are right to think that technology has huge implications for education. But no more with the computer than with the television will the decisive problem be one of familiarization and adaptation. The adaptation occurs all too well on its own. Children must learn, rather, how to hold these technologies in a human balance. And I suggest that a bird in the hand—and a pinecone, and a rock, and a crawdad, and a snowflake—are the counterbalances we need if our alienation from nature is not to become more than the world can bear. These bits of nature may not seem like much to us—but that is the problem. For the child they hold magic—exactly the magic that, in a matured form, may be required to ground the adult in a twenty-first century of encompassing virtuality.

(1998)

ERIK REECE

THE SCHOOLS WE NEED

When public education fails, democracy fails with it

IT'S A COLD DECEMBER EVENING in Lexington, Kentucky, and I'm sitting by the fire with a teetering stack of final essays from ENG 104: Freshman Comp. I know what I'm in for. All semester I've been hectoring my fifty-odd students to insert commas after introductory phrases, to improve paragraph development, and to remember that the phrase *for granted* (as in "take for granted") means "to accept," whereas *for granite*, the phrase they often use instead, could only suggest homage to that igneous rock, something akin to W. H. Auden's poem "In Praise of Limestone."

It's been a tough three months. I had been away from full-time teaching for a few years, and away from eighteen-year-olds for longer. From 1995 to 2005, I taught four, sometimes five, sections of Freshman Comp each semester. I read roughly 8,000 essays during that decade—200,000 pages, 50,000,000 words. After all that, I took a little time off to do some writing of my own. But when my book was finished, the department chair ordered me back to the front line.

And Freshman Comp *is* the front line. All incoming college students take it, and their numbers are on the rise. Consequently, we are legion as well, we writing teachers, we circlers of the comma splice, we well-intentioned, underpaid masses. Despite what you may have heard, we are not covert operatives, Maoist holdovers who have infiltrated the ranks of higher education. While I do have major concerns about the predatory nature of corporate capitalism, as I imagine many of us do by now, my motives, like those of my colleagues, are mostly pure. Our goals can be simply stated if not easily achieved. Namely, we want to teach your children to think for themselves and to communicate those thoughts through effective use of language.

Of course, unless you are a Dadaist poet, you have to write about *something*. But after reading thousands of essays (a noun I much prefer to "arguments") about abortion, gun control, and gay rights—all important issues—I decided that, on my return to Freshman Comp, I would ask my freshmen to essay (a verb I prefer to "argue") on a topic they all presumably knew something about: high school. I began with a simple prompt for the first essay: evaluate the education you received over the last four years.

Next I asked my students to write profiles of their best or worst teachers. They seemed to like this, largely because it gave them a chance to vent some pent-up spleen and settle some scores, at least on paper. I noticed that most students chose to describe the poor teachers and to enumerate their many flaws. Very few—and these were mostly students from parochial schools—chose to profile a good teacher.

After that exercise, I asked my freshmen to describe assignments, curricula, class discussions, and books they had liked or disliked. I told them that writing is a movement back and forth between observation and insight. I said: first describe a thing in detail—a person, a place, an experience—then let that description lead to some insight, some take-away value. That's what readers want, I emphasized, to get something out of what they have read. I told my students to try to think of me not as the teacher who would affix grades to their essays, but as an ordinary reader who was interested—which I was, and am—in what goes on these days in American high schools.

What I ended up taking away was pretty grim, both on the content level and with regard to the writing itself. In terms of content, this is the picture that emerged from those fifty essays:

- Many teachers show no passion for their subjects.

- Many teachers don't seem to know their subjects very well.

- Teachers often have very low expectations for their students and very lax standards (late work is rarely penalized).

- Many teachers are afraid to engage students in real critical thinking or actual dialogue; they simply rely on handouts and lectures.

- Assignments don't seem relevant to students' "real" lives.

- Many teachers only "teach to the test."

- The majority of the work is far too easy and leads to boredom.

- Students express an overwhelming feeling that only their attendance and test scores are important to teachers and administrators.

I am obviously drawing these conclusions from wholly anecdotal evidence. But because the uniformity of that evidence was so overwhelming, I think it deserves some serious consideration. There were exceptions. Almost everyone could produce at least one example of a good or great teacher from high school, someone who inspired or stirred intellectual curiosity. But overall, my students described days of endless worksheets, lifeless lectures, and an impenetrable fog of boredom.

After reading all of these existential scenarios, I decided to hand out an essay by John Taylor Gatto called "Against School: How public education cripples our kids, and why." A career New York City schoolteacher, Gatto argues that students are bored because they are *supposed* to be. The education system is intentionally designed to shape them into a passive mass who will, in bovine fashion, join the labor force and become unthinking mass producers and mass consumers. Public education, in Gatto's estimation, is a scheme dreamed up by the captains of industry to incubate servility and ultimately sabotage anything like a real democracy. I don't think my classes quite bought into Gatto's conspiracy theory ("yeah . . . maybe . . . whatever"), but they did agree that the American high school classroom is pretty damn dull.

What concerned me as much as my students' disdain for their teachers, though, was the quality of their writing. Potential ideas lay dormant and undeveloped on the page; basic rules of grammar and punctuation went unheeded; logic was all but absent. After reading that first round of essays, I began annoying my friends with dire, unprovoked brooding on the dismal state of high school education in this country. More than one friend warned me against committing what I have come to call the *Breakfast Club* fallacy. In that flawed, but seminal, '80s high school film, the assistant

principal is complaining to Janitor Carl that the kids have
changed, gone bad, turned on him. "Bullshit," replies Carl.
"The kids haven't changed. You have." That's the *Breakfast
Club* fallacy: the kids aren't getting worse; I'm just getting
older and more cantankerous.

Maybe so. My own high school was hardly a proving
ground for intellectual inquiry. Still, I'm concerned, and for
the same reasons that led George Orwell to write the essay
"Politics and the English Language": bad writing leads to bad
thinking, and vice versa; uncritical acceptance of others' preju-
dices can lead to people marching around with signs display-
ing Hitler mustaches on an African-American president. In
fact, the entire faith we put in democracy as a form of govern-
ance rests on the fragile assumption that, in the realm of free
and open debate, conscientious thought will more often than
not carry the day. And that assumption, as Thomas Jefferson
saw more clearly than the other founding fathers, rests in turn
on a viable system of public education.

Citizen education "was the central, defining moment of
[Jefferson's] political and moral philosophy," wrote political
theorist Benjamin Barber. "Everything else turned on it."
Throughout his correspondence, Jefferson maintained that
only an educated citizenry can practice true self-governance,
and toward that end he drafted the 1779 Virginia Bill for
the More General Diffusion of Knowledge, the first piece
of legislation in the young country to propose at least three
years of primary education for both boys and girls. However,
the bill failed, and in many respects, American public education continues to fail the Jeffersonian dream of emancipa-
tory learning. Only now it fails in the face of a climate crisis,
unsustainable resource use, and rising world populations. It
fails at a time when the stakes concerning public education
have never been higher.

Writer and teacher David Orr, author of the environmental education classic *Ecological Literacy*, has observed that too often in this country, education has only served to make Americans "better vandals," uncritical consumers and exploiters of the natural world. While pundits like Thomas Friedman lament that American children are falling behind in science and math, rarely do we hear that they are being woefully ill-prepared for the arts of citizenship and stewardship—dispositions that will be every bit as necessary on Friedman's hot and crowded planet. If we want to preserve democracy in America, radical and widespread changes in the way we educate American children and teenagers must begin at once.

Politicians in Washington have spent decades disparaging American public schools as too far gone, too decrepit to bother resuscitating. But as I look back over my students' list of grievances concerning their own high school educations, it strikes me that none of these problems seems at all intractable. As with other American crises, such as energy policy, tax reform, and drug sentencing, the problem doesn't seem to be a lack of solutions, but rather an absence of will. My students' complaints, largely about the classroom environment and the content of the curriculum, can be clustered into three groups: quality of teaching, expectations placed on students, and relevance of subject matter to that much-contested realm they call "real life."

As someone who has spent nearly twenty years in writing classrooms with late-adolescent Americans, I'd like to take a crack at this list. But before I do, it's necessary to say a few words about the students themselves. At the risk of generalizing, it seems to me that two of the more serious problems afflicting American adolescents today are the fear of not fitting in and an astonishing lack of curiosity about the world beyond their cell phones. Popular culture instills high levels of passivity among its most vulnerable targets, the young. There is, to take one pervasive example, not a single item for sale at my local mall that asks the consumer to do something, make something, or master a skill (the store that sold telescopes and chess sets recently closed). Yet American teenagers have on average one hundred dollars a week of disposable income, which they typically spend at the mall. What they consume helps them adopt an easy, off-the-rack persona, but it does little to cultivate real self-invention, the unfolding of one's nature that Emerson called the "chief end of man." This passive shaping of the self leads, I think, to a flimsy narcissism that results in a lack of curiosity about the world outside the self: real life.

A neighbor who is a longtime high school English teacher told me recently, "When these kids get to you, they won't have learned a damn thing about writing. All I do in class is police." Like my neighbor, many of us assume that the American youth have become captive to popular culture. Certainly this makes teaching much harder today—probably harder than it's ever been—but it also seems like an opportunity to contest the ground we as educators have yielded too quickly to the entertainment industry. Instead of allowing the practice of accumulation to replace authentic experience, we should be creating opportunities for our students to learn how to more fully inhabit their own lives and the larger world.

Which brings me back to the teachers. The first charge: *teachers show no passion for their subjects and they don't seem to know their subjects very well.* I would wager, along with my students, that many teachers show little passion for their subjects precisely because they don't know them very well, or as well as they might. For this reason, some critics have proposed abolishing entirely the education departments at all American universities. I understand this sentiment. About half of my writing students are education majors, and I hear endless complaints about busywork and irrelevant assignments. One student stayed in school an extra year to earn a minor in Appalachian studies so, she told me, "I would actually know something worth teaching."

But if we do not take on the rather cumbersome task of dismantling ed schools, we should at least insist that prospective teachers *major* in the subjects they plan to teach. That would be the most immediate and dramatic way to increase teachers' knowledge of their subject and, presumably, their passion for it. Nothing I have found, or have observed while mentoring new teachers, inspires more confidence in front of a class than mastery of the material. Teenagers are like hyenas in their ability to sniff out uncertainty and fear in an instructor; quickly they can turn into an unruly pack, and it becomes almost impossible to regain their respect or decorum. Knowledge of and passion for one's subject represents the surest way for teachers to keep students interested and engaged. Conversely, someone with no passion for a subject should simply not be teaching it.

When I was a freshman in college, I took a foreign film class that was way over my head. One day, after watching Fellini's *The Clowns*, the professor—a tall Cuban-American of some bearing—fell back against the chalkboard and said, "If you don't cry at the end of *The Clowns*, you are not a human being!" I hadn't cried. In fact, I hadn't really understood the film. But I wanted to feel—about anything—what my professor felt about *The Clowns*. It wasn't Fellini, but the teacher's passion for Fellini, that moved and inspired me and that I recall to this day.

Now for the charge that *teachers have low expectations and the work is too easy*. Anyone who has ever hosted a European exchange student knows this to be true, relative to expectations placed on students overseas. The logical solution is to assign work that is more challenging and treat students more like adults who have to navigate a world of ethical uncertainty and information overload.

If the popular culture is cajoling adolescents to be unthinking, passive consumers, teachers must meet that message with an active, critical response. For instance, we might ask the girls to bring to class a magazine they read and the boys to do likewise. We might ask: What are the messages in every ad in your magazine? How are the messages to girls different from the messages to boys? Can the products deliver on their promises? What percentage of those promises seem true? Do those percentages differ according to gender? All are basic questions. But they will yield crucial information about gender and identity in this country, and teenage students will gain that knowledge through the use of analytical skills that can be applied in other fields.

I suspect the hesitancy by many high school teachers to hold active class discussions about real moral and ethical dilemmas may be a byproduct of how contested and politicized the word *values* has become. No one wants to talk about them because someone might become offended, or someone might say the wrong thing, or the messiness of open debate might get exposed.

A few years ago, on the first day of my Freshman Comp class, an argument broke out over whether or not "Redskins" was a racist name for a professional football team. I hadn't expected or planned this debate, but I let it rage for half the class, trying to direct and redirect the lines of argument as best I could. It seemed like productive chaos, and afterward, the class did not emerge from the debate divided, but rather heartened, it seemed, that everyone had been given a chance to voice diverse opinions. Something important happened that day: the students created a democratic space in which to debate and consider ideas. It wasn't because of anything I did, but simply because I didn't get in the way of the students' own grappling over questions of perspective, personal background, and the ability of words to both empower and harm.

And with that, I have already veered into my students' third charge, that *high school subject matter isn't relevant to real life*. This sentiment seems to be grounded in the suspicion that, because school budgets and salaries are determined by test scores, many teachers are simply "covering the material" in a perfunctory way, or, even more insidiously, "teaching to the test." Neither exercise seems like real learning to adolescents, who immediately sense its contrived nature and, as a result, retain little of that knowledge from year to year. Many progressive educators have responded by pushing for a curriculum that encourages more depth than breadth. That is to say, cover less material, but examine it in ways that promote real inquiry and understanding on the part of the students.

Deborah Meier, a senior scholar at NYU's Steinhardt School of Education and a founder of the Coalition of Essential Schools, suggests that we replace the cover-the-material mode of teaching by cultivating a "habit of mind" that can be applied to *all* material. Such a habit nurtures the intellectual skills students need to make decisions on complex matters and is based on such things as: quality of evidence (how do we know it's true?), consideration of various viewpoints (how would it look through someone else's eyes?), the search for patterns and causes (what are the consequences?), and relevance (who cares?). These criteria will serve students well on any standardized test because they will have been taught how to evaluate the evidence before them, regardless of what it may be. And Meier's last question, "who cares?" speaks directly to my students' complaint about the relevancy of subject matter, because their demand for assignments that are relevant to real life does have merit. In the year 2011, real life can be quite scary, and helping students to navigate it requires a much more challenging curriculum.

When deregulated corporations destroy entire ecosystems and the Supreme Court grants those same corporations more "rights" to express themselves as "persons" (very rich persons), the need for a more Jeffersonian form of schooling— one that emphasizes serious critical inquiry in the service of citizenship—is imperative to the future of democracy. We need schools, as novelist Mark Slouka recently wrote, that produce "men and women capable of furthering what's best about us and forestalling what's worst."

The good news is we can begin revitalizing both education and democracy by implementing a curriculum that incubates what I will call the "citizen-self." As teachers, I believe our purpose should be twofold: 1) to provide the opportunity for individual self-invention among students, and 2) to create a space where that individual takes on the role and the responsibility of the social citizen. The pedagogy I have in mind combines the Romantic idea of the *bildung*, the cultivation of one's own intellectual and psychological nature, with the Pragmatist view that such individuality must be vigorously protected by acts of citizenship. That is to say, it encourages Deborah Meier's "habit of mind" toward the goal of helping each student determine what she or he truly thinks and feels about an issue or an idea, and it encourages what psychologist and philosopher William James called a "habit of action," a way of translating such thinking into citizenship. At the risk of oversimplifying, we might say that the first part cultivates the inner self, while the second shapes the outer self. But these two selves cannot be separated; each depends upon and strengthens the other.

Thomas Jefferson believed that the fundamental American impulse of this citizen-self should be anti-industrial, anti-corporation, and should cultivate a generalist approach to education and work. Jefferson also believed that both politics and education best succeed at the local level. This has proven true time and again in my own experience. In the Kentucky River watershed, at the headwaters of this ecosystem in the central Appalachian region of eastern Kentucky, some of the most fascinating chapters of this country's history have been written, often in blood. Here, Aunt Molly Jackson (the "Pistol Packin' Mama") held up a coal company store and stole flour to feed starving children, here men and women stood up to strip miners whose bulldozers threatened their own land, and here country music got invented. Central Appalachia also happens to be the most biologically diverse ecosystem in North America. Yet most adolescents (and most adults) in my watershed know little or nothing about the ecosystem, the coal camps, or the blasting apart of the east Kentucky mountains; they listen to Brad Paisley and Taylor Swift instead of native singers like Loretta Lynn and Jean Ritchie.

My point isn't necessarily that Jean Ritchie's music is better than Brad Paisley's (though it is), but that when students learn about artists from their particular watersheds, they begin to feel their own home place legitimated, validated. Localizing knowledge makes the curriculum more relevant to students' own experience, and it can instill a sense of pride about the places where our students live. "When I was growing up in these mountains," wrote Kentucky novelist Lee Smith, "I was always taught that culture was someplace else, and that when the time came, I'd be sent off to get some. Now everybody here realizes that we don't have to go anyplace else to 'get culture'—we've got our own, and we've had it all along."

Taking pride in one's place can also lead to a desire to take responsibility for that place, which is, after all, the crux of citizenship. Teachers can foster this impulse by focusing assignments on local issues, allowing chemistry, biology, English, and civics classes to be driven by a problem-solving impulse. Such learning is inevitably interdisciplinary because real problems, and real learning, rarely break down along clear disciplinary lines. If a strip mine is polluting a local source of drinking water, that is clearly a biological and chemical problem, but it is also an ethical problem grounded in lessons of history. To solve it, many fields of knowledge must be brought to bear. And to articulate the solution will require some skilled rhetoric indeed. Working to solve that problem becomes at once an experiment in stewardship (the opposite of vandalism) and citizenship (participatory democracy).

It also goes some distance toward breaking down the artificial, but very real, wall between school and life, between learning and doing. The rejection of this false dichotomy was one of the primary goals of the American Pragmatist educators like John Dewey and Jane Addams. Of the turn-of-the-century settlement school movement, Addams wrote that it "stands for application as opposed to research, for emotion as opposed to abstraction, for universal interest as opposed to specialization." Specialization has, too often, been the enemy of educating the citizen-self. It encourages careerism as the only goal of education, and its narrowness can result in an abdication of responsibility concerning problems that lie outside of one's specialty. These narrowly focused specialists can cause problems. Financial specialists caused the economic collapse, genetic specialists have created crops that require far more pesticide application, and we don't yet know the full havoc caused by deep-water drilling specialists. But as we saw with BP's cagey initial reaction to the Gulf disaster, as well as Monsanto's outrageous contempt for farmers and seed-savers, specialization also seems to create a troubling loss of empathy.

Empathy, what Jane Addams called emotion, has largely disappeared from American public life. Our politics and punditry are too divisive, the gap between rich and poor too wide, the messages from the media too preoccupied with what William James called "the bitch-goddess SUCCESS." We think of public life as a playing field of winners and losers, when we should be thinking about it, to borrow from Dewey, as a single organism made up of thousands of single but interconnected cells—a whole that needs all of its parts, working cooperatively. In other words, we should be thinking about how our educational institutions can be geared less toward competitiveness and more toward turning out graduates who feel a responsibility toward their places and their peers.

Here is the crux of the matter: As we enter an era of dwindling resources and potential mass migration due to climate change, we are going to need much more empathy—perhaps more than ever before—if we hope to retain our humanity. Empathy must be the measure of our students', and our own, emotional and ethical maturity.

If my English-teaching neighbor is right, and she is simply policing student behavior until graduation, then John Taylor Gatto is also right that we are simply warehousing students in public schools until they are old enough, as the Steve Earle song goes, to "walk into the county bank and sign away your life." That might have been Alexander Hamilton's idea of the American Dream—making bankers rich—but it's not what Thomas Jefferson envisioned for the country. Nor is it in the best interest of its citizens.

When someone asked Benjamin Franklin what type of

government he and the other founders had birthed on this country, he famously replied, "A republic, if you can keep it." The truth is that we have not kept it. We have relinquished it to Wall Street bankers and corporations that spend $6 billion a year to ensure that political hirelings do their bidding. As a result, the United States has the largest income gap of any country in the Northern Hemisphere (it is also, according to the 2009 census, the largest income gap in this country's history). The problem with this, as epidemiologists Richard Wilkinson and Kate Picket have found, is that every single societal problem, with no exceptions, can be tied directly to income inequality. As a result, the U.S. has higher levels of mental illness, infant mortality, obesity, violence, incarceration, and substance abuse than any other country north of the equator. And we have the worst environmental record on the planet. If this is a republic, you can have it.

How do we recover, how do we reinvent, the country that Jefferson and Franklin envisioned? We must become better citizens, and that transformation must begin—and really can only begin—in better public schools.

Putting my students in situations where they might learn and practice the art of real democracy has become a large part of my own teaching, and it is with these goals in mind that I often take them to a place in eastern Kentucky called Robinson Forest. It is a brilliant remnant of the mixed mesophytic ecosystem, and it is home to the cleanest streams in the state. Yet only a short walk away from our base camp you can watch those streams die, literally turn lifeless, because of the mountaintop removal strip mining that is happening all around Robinson Forest.

A few years ago, I had one student (I'll call him Brian) who had only signed up for one of my classes because it fit his schedule. He was, in his own words, "a right-wing nut job," and he disagreed with virtually everything I said in class. But he was funny and respectful and I liked having him around. On our class trip to Robinson Forest, we all hiked up out of the forest to a fairly typical mountaintop removal site. The hard-packed dirt and rock was completely barren, save for a few non-native, scrubby grasses. To call this post-mined land a "moonscape," as many do, is an insult to the moon.

Brian was quiet as we walked, and then he asked, "When are they going to reclaim this land?"

"It has been reclaimed," I said. "They sprayed hydro-seed, so now this qualifies as wildlife habitat."

"This is it?"

"This is all the law requires."

Brian went quiet again, until finally he said, "This is awful."

Then he asked, "What do you think would happen if every University of Kentucky student came to see this?"

I pulled the old teacher trick and turned the question back on him: "What do *you* think would happen?"

Brian paused, and then said, "I think mountaintop removal would end."

(2011)

BRENDA PETERSON

ANIMAL ALLIES

"My imaginary friend really lived once," the teenage girl began, head bent, her fingers twisting her long red hair. She stood in the circle of other adolescents gathered in my Seattle Arts and Lectures storytelling class at the summer Seattle Academy. Here were kids from all over the city—every color and class, all strangers one to another. Over the next two weeks we would become a fierce tribe, telling our own and our tribe's story. Our first assignment was to introduce our imaginary friends from childhood. This shy fourteen-year-old girl, Sarah, had struck me on the first day because she always sat next to me, as if under my wing, and though her freckles and stylish clothes suggested she was a popular girl, her demeanor showed the detachment of someone deeply preoccupied. She never met my eye, nor did she join in the first few days of storytelling when the ten boys and four girls were regaling one another with futuristic characters called Shiva and Darshon, Masters of the Universe. So far the story lines we'd imagined were more Pac-Man than drama. After the first two days I counted a legion of characters killed off in intergalactic battle. The settings for all these stories portrayed the earth as an environmental wasteland, a ruined shell hardly shelter to anything animal or human. One of the girls called herself Nero the White Wolf and wandered the blackened tundra howling her powerful despair; another girl was a unicorn whose horn always told the truth. All the stories were full of plagues and nuclear wars—even though this is the generation that has witnessed the fall of the Berlin Wall, the end of the Cold War. Their imaginations have been shaped by a childhood story line that anticipates the end of this world.

After three days of stories set on an earth besieged by disease and barren of nature, I made a rule: No more characters or animals could die this first week. I asked if someone might imagine a living world, one that survives even our species.

It was on this third day of group storytelling that Sarah jumped into the circle and told her story:

"My imaginary friend is called Angel now because she's in heaven, but her real name was Katie," Sarah began. "She was my best friend from fourth to tenth grade. She had freckles like me and brown hair and more boyfriends—sometimes five at a time—because Katie said, 'I *like* to be confused!' She was a real sister too and we used to say we'd be friends for life. . . ." Sarah stopped, gave me a furtive glance and then gulped in a great breath of air like someone drowning, about to go down. Her eyes fixed inward, her voice dropped to a monotone. "Then one day last year, Katie and I were walking home from school and a red sports car came up behind us. Someone yelled, 'Hey, Katie!' She turned . . . and he blew her head off. A bullet grazed my skull, too, and I blacked out. When I woke up, Katie was gone, dead forever." Sarah stopped, stared down at her feet and murmured in that same terrible monotone, "Cops never found her murderer, case is closed."

All the kids shifted and took a deep breath, although Sarah herself was barely breathing at all. "Let's take some time to write," I told the kids and put on a cello concerto for them to

listen to while they wrote. As they did their assignment, the
kids glanced over surreptitiously at Sarah, who sat staring at
her hands in her lap.

I did not know what to do with her story; she had offered
it to a group of kids she had known but three days. It explained her self-imposed exile during lunch hours and while
waiting for the bus. All I knew was that she'd brought this
most important story of her life into the circle of storytellers
and it could not be ignored as if *she* were a case to be closed.
This story lived in her, would define and shape her young life.
Because she had given it to us, we needed to witness and re-
ceive—and perhaps tell it back to her in the ancient tradition
of tribal call and response.

"Listen," I told the group as the cello faded and they
looked up from their work. "We're going to talk story the way
they used to long ago when people sat around at night in
circles just like this one. That was a time when we still listened to animals and trees and didn't think ourselves so alone
in this world. Now we're going to carry out jungle justice and
find Katie's killer. We'll call him before our tribe. All right?
Who wants to begin the story?"

All the Shivas and Darshons and Masters of the Universe
volunteered to be heroes on this quest. Nero the White Wolf
asked to be a scout. Unicorn, with.her truth-saying horn,
was declared judge. Another character joined the hunt: Fish,
whose translucent belly was a shining "soul mirror" that could
reveal one's true nature to anyone who looked into it.

A fierce commander of this hunt was Rat, whose army of
computerized comrades could read brain waves and call down
lightning lasers as weapons. Rat began the questioning and
performed the early detective work. Katie, speaking from beyond the earth, as Sarah put it, gave us other facts. We learned
that two weeks before Katie's murder, one of her boyfriends

was shot outside a restaurant by a man in the same red car—another driveby death. So Sarah had not only seen her best friend killed at her side, but she had also walked out into a parking lot to find Katie leaning over her boyfriend's body. For Sarah, it had been two murders by age thirteen.

With the help of our myriad computer-character legions were determined that the murderer was a man named Carlos, a drug lord who used local gangs to deal cocaine. At a party Carlos had misinterpreted Katie's videotaping her friends dancing as witnessing a big drug deal. For that, Rat said, "This dude decides Katie's to go down. So yo, man, he offs her without a second thought."

Bad dude, indeed, this Carlos. And who was going to play Carlos now that all the tribe knew his crime? I took on the role, and as I told my story I felt my face hardening into a contempt that carried me far away from these young pursuers, deep into the Amazon jungle where Rat and his computer armies couldn't follow, where all their space-age equipment had to be shed until there was only hand-tohand simple fate.

In the Amazon, the kids changed without effort, in an easy shape-shifting to their animal selves. Suddenly there were no more Masters of the Universe with intergalactic weapons—there was instead Jaguar and Snake, Fish and Pink Dolphin. There was powerful claw and all-knowing serpent, there was Fish who could grow big and small, and a dolphin whose sonar saw past the skin. We were now a tribe of animals, pawing, running, invisible in our jungle, eyes shining in the night, seeing Carlos as he canoed the mighty river, laughing because he did not know he had animals tracking him.

All through the story, I'd kept my eye on Sarah who played the role of her dead friend. The detachment I'd first seen in her was in fact the deadness Sarah carried, the violence that had hollowed her out inside, the friend who haunted her imagination. But now her face was alive, responding to each animal's report of tracking Carlos. She hung on the words, looking suddenly very young, like a small girl eagerly awaiting her turn to enter the circling jump rope.

"I'm getting away from you," I said, snarling as I'd imagined Carlos would. I paddled my canoe and gave a harsh laugh, "I'll escape, easy!" "No!" Sarah shouted. "Let *me* tell it!"

"Tell it!" her tribe shouted. "Well, Carlos only thinks he's escaping," Sarah smiled, waving her hands. "He's escaped from so many he's harmed before. But I call out 'FISH!' And Fish comes. He swims alongside the canoe and grows bigger, bigger until at last Carlos turns and sees this HUGE river monster swimming right alongside him and that man is afraid because suddenly Fish turns his belly up to Carlos's face. Fish forces him to look into that soul mirror. Carlos *sees* everyone he's ever killed and all the people who loved them and got left behind. And Carlos sees Katie and me and what he's done to us. He sees everything and he knows his soul is black. And he really doesn't want to die now because he knows then he'll stare into his soul mirror forever. But Fish makes him keep looking until Carlos starts screaming he's sorry, he's so sorry. Then...Fish *eats* him!"

The animals roared and cawed and congratulated Sarah for calling Fish to mirror a murderer's soul before taking jungle justice. Class had ended, but no one wanted to leave. We wanted to stay in our jungle, stay within our animals—and so we did. I asked them to close their eyes and call their animals to accompany them home. I told them that some South American tribes believe that when you are born, an animal is born with you. This animal protects and lives alongside you even if it's far away in an Amazon jungle—it came into the world at the same time you did. And, I told them, it dies with you to guide you back into the spirit world.

The kids decided to go home and make animal masks, returning the next day wearing the faces of their chosen animal. When they came into class the next day it was as if we never left the Amazon. Someone dimmed the lights, there were drawings everywhere of jaguars and chimps and snakes. Elaborate masks had replaced the Masters of the Universe who began this tribal journey. We sat behind our masks in a circle with the lights low and there was an acute, alert energy running between us, as eyes met behind animal faces.

I realize that I, who grew up in the forest wild, who first memorized the earth with my hands, have every reason to feel this familiar animal resonance. But many of these teenagers have barely been in the woods; in fact, many inner city kids are *afraid* of nature. They would not willingly sign up for an Outward Bound program or backpacking trek; they don't think about recycling in a world they believe already ruined and in their imaginations abandoned for intergalactic nomad futures. These kids are not environmentalists who worry about saving nature. And yet, when imagining an Amazon forest too thick for weapons to penetrate, too primitive for their futuristic Pac-Man battles, they return instinctively to their animal selves. These are animals they have only seen in zoos or on television, yet there is a profound identification, an ease of inhabiting another species that portends great hope for our own species's survival. Not because nature is "out there" to be saved or sanctioned, but because nature is *in* them. The ancient, green world has never left us though we have long ago left the forest.

What happens when we call upon our inner landscape to connect with the living rainforests still left in the natural world? I believe our imagination can be as mutually nurturing as an umbilical cord between our bodies and the planet. As we told our Amazon stories over the next week of class,

gathered in a circle of animal masks, we could feel the rainforest growing in that sterile classroom. Lights low, surrounded
by serpents, the jaguar clan, the elephants, I'd as often hear
growls, hisses, and howls as words. Between this little classroom and the vast Amazon rainforest stretched a fine thread
of story that grew thicker each day, capable of carrying our
jungle meditations.

When Elephant stood in the circle and said simply, "My
kind are dying out," there was outrage from the other animals. "We'll stop those poachers!" cried Rat and Chimp. "We'll
call Jaguar clan to protect you." And they did.

This protection is of a kind that reaches the other side
of the world. Children's imagination is a primal force, just
as strong as lobbying efforts and boycotts and endangered
species acts. When children claim another species as not only
their imaginary friend, but also as the animal within them—
their ally—doesn't that change the outer world?

This class believes it to be so. They may be young, but
their memories and alliances with the animals are very old.
By telling their own animal stories they are practicing ecology
at its most profound and healing level. Story as ecology—it's
so simple, something we've forgotten. In our environmental
wars the emphasis has been on saving species, not *becoming*
them. We've fallen into an environmental fundamentalism
that calls down hellfire and brimstone on the evil polluters
and self-righteously struts about protecting other species as if
we are gods who can save their souls.

But the animals' souls are not in our hands. Only our own
souls are within our ken. It is our own spiritual relationship
to animals that must evolve. Any change begins with imagining ourselves in a new way. And who has preserved their
imaginations as a natural resource most deeply? Not adults,
who so often have strip-mined their dreams and imagination

for material dross. Those who sit behind the wheel of a Jaguar have probably forgotten the wild, black cat that first ran with them as children. Imagination is relegated to nighttime dreams, which are then dismissed in favor of "the real world." But children, like some adults, know that the real world stretches farther than what we can see-that's why they shift easily between visions of our tribal past and our future worlds. The limits of the adult world are there for these teenagers, but they still have a foot in the vast inner magic of childhood. It is this magical connection I called upon when I asked the kids to do the Dance of the Animals.

The day of the big dance I awoke with a sharp pain at my right eye. Seems my Siamese, who has always slept draped around my head, had stretched and his claw caught the corner of my eye. In the mirror I saw a two-inch scratch streaking from my eye like jungle make-up or a primitive face painting. "The mark of the wildcat," the kids pronounced it when I walked into the dimly lit room to be met by a circle of familiar creatures. Never in ten years had my Siamese scratched my face. I took it as a sign that the dance began in his animal dream.

I put on my cobra mask and hissed a greeting to Chimp, Rat, Jaguar, and Unicorn. Keen eyes tracked me from behind colorful masks. I held up my rain stick which was also our talking stick and called the creatures one by one into the circle. "Sister Snake!" I called. "Begin the dance!"

Slowly, in rhythm to the deep, bell-like beat of my Northwest Native drum, each animal entered the circle and soon the dance sounded like this: Boom, step, twirl, and slither and stalk and snarl and chirp and caw, caw. Glide, glow, growl, and whistle and howl and shriek and trill and hiss, hiss. Each dance was distinct-from the undulating serpent on his belly, to the dainty high hoofing of Unicorn, from the syncopated stomps of Chimp on all-fours to Rat's covert jitterbug behind the stalking half-dark Jaguar. We danced, and the humid, lush jungle filled this room.

In that story line stretching between us and the Amazon, we connected with those animals and their spirits. And in return, we were complete—with animals as soul mirrors. We remembered who we were, by allowing the animals inside us to survive.

The dance is not over as long as we have our animal partners. When the kids left our last class, they still wore their masks fiercely. I was told that even on the bus they stayed deep in their animal character. I like to imagine those strong, young animals out there now in this wider jungle. I believe that Rat will survive the inner-city gangs; that Chimp will find his characteristic comedy even as his parents deal with divorce; I hope that Unicorn will always remember her mystical truth-telling horn. And as for Sarah who joined the Jaguar clan, elected as the first girl-leader over much mutinous boy-growling—Sarah knows the darkness she stalks and the nightmares that stalk her. She has animal eyes to see, to find even a murderer. She reminded me as she left the jungle that she could still see in the dark. Taking her catlike, graceful leave, she handed me a poem she'd written; it was signed, "Jaguar—future poet."

(1993)

RICHARD LOUV

LEAVE NO CHILD INSIDE

The growing movement to reconnect children and nature

AS A BOY, I pulled out dozens—perhaps hundreds—of survey stakes in a vain effort to slow the bulldozers that were taking out my woods to make way for a new subdivision. Had I known then what I've since learned from a developer, that I should have simply moved the stakes around to be more effective, I would surely have done that too. So you might imagine my dubiousness when, a few weeks after the publication of my 2005 book, *Last Child in the Woods*, I received an e-mail from Derek Thomas, who introduced himself as vice chairman and chief investment officer of Newland Communities, one of the nation's largest privately owned residential development companies. "I have been reading your new book," he wrote, "and am profoundly disturbed by some of the information you present."

Thomas said he wanted to do something positive. He invited me to an envisioning session in Phoenix to "explore how Newland can improve or redefine our approach to open space preservation and the interaction between our home-buyers and nature." A few weeks later, in a conference room filled with about eighty developers, builders, and real estate marketers, I offered my sermonette. The folks in the crowd were partially responsible for the problem, I suggested, because they destroy natural habitat, design communities in ways that discourage any real contact with nature, and include covenants that virtually criminalize outdoor play—outlawing tree-climbing, fort-building, even chalk-drawing on sidewalks.

I was ready to make a fast exit when Thomas, a bearded man with an avuncular demeanor, stood up and said, "I want you all to go into small groups and solve the problem: how are we going to build communities in the future that actually connect kids with nature?" The room filled with noise and excitement. By the time the groups reassembled to report the ideas they had generated, I had glimpsed the primal power of connecting children and nature: it can inspire unexpected advocates and lure unlikely allies to enter an entirely new place. Call it the doorway effect. Once through the door, they can revisualize seemingly intractable problems and produce solutions they might otherwise never have imagined.

A half hour after Thomas's challenge, the groups reported their ideas. Among them: leave some land and native habitat in place (that's a good start); employ green design principles; incorporate nature trails and natural waterways; throw out the conventional covenants and restrictions that discourage or prohibit natural play and rewrite the rules to encourage it; allow kids to build forts and tree houses or plant gardens; and create small, on-site nature centers.

"Kids could become guides, using cell phones, along nature trails that lead to schools at the edge of the development," someone suggested. Were the men and women in this room just blowing smoke? Maybe. Developers exploiting our hunger for nature, I thought, *just as they market their subdivisions by naming their streets after the trees and streams that they destroy.* But the fact that developers, builders, and real estate marketers would approach Derek Thomas's question with such apparently heartfelt enthusiasm was revealing. The quality of their ideas mattered less than the fact that they had them. While they may not get there themselves, the people in this room were visualizing a very different future. They were undergoing a process of discovery that has proliferated around the country in the past two years, and not only among developers.

For decades, environmental educators, conservationists, and others have worked, often heroically, to bring more children to nature—usually with inadequate support from policymakers. A number of trends, including the recent unexpected national media attention to *Last Child* and "nature-deficit disorder," have now brought the concerns of these veteran advocates before a broader audience. While some may argue that the word "movement" is hyperbole, we do seem to have reached a tipping point. State and regional campaigns, sometimes called Leave No Child Inside, have begun to form in Cincinnati, Cleveland, Chicago, the San Francisco Bay Area, St. Louis, Connecticut, Florida, Colorado, Texas, and elsewhere. A host of related initiatives—among them the simple-living, walkable-cities, nature-education, and land-trust movements—have begun to find common cause, and collective strength, through this issue. The activity has attracted a diverse assortment of people who might otherwise never work together.

In September 2006, the National Conservation Training Center and the Conservation Fund hosted the National Dialogue on Children and Nature in Shepherdstown, West Virginia. The conference drew some 350 people from around the country, representing educators, health-care experts, recreation companies, residential developers, urban planners, conservation agencies, academics, and other groups. Even the Walt Disney Company was represented. Support has also come from religious leaders, liberal and conservative, who understand that all spiritual life begins with a sense of wonder, and that one of the first windows to wonder is the natural world. "Christians should take the lead in reconnecting with nature and disconnecting from machines," writes R. Albert Mohler Jr., president of the Southern Baptist Theological Seminary, the flagship school of the Southern Baptist Convention.

To some extent, the movement is fueled by organizational or economic self-interest. But something deeper is going on here. With its nearly universal appeal, this issue seems to hint at a more atavistic motivation. It may have something to do with what Harvard professor E. O. Wilson calls the biophilia hypothesis, which is that human beings are innately attracted to nature: biologically, we are all still hunters and gatherers, and there is something in us, which we do not fully understand, that needs an occasional immersion in nature. We do know that when people talk about the disconnect between children and nature—if they are old enough to remember a time when outdoor play was the norm—they almost always tell stories about their own childhoods: this tree house or fort, that special woods or ditch or creek or meadow. They recall those "places of initiation," in the words of naturalist Bob Pyle, where they may have first sensed with awe and wonder the largeness of the world seen and unseen. When people share these stories, their cultural, political, and religious walls come tumbling down.

And when that happens, ideas can pour forth—and lead to ever more insightful approaches. It's a short conceptual leap, for example, from the notions generated by Derek Thomas's working group to the creation of a truly sustainable development like the pioneering Village Homes, in Davis, California, where suburban homes are pointed inward toward open green space, vegetable gardens are encouraged, and orchards, not gates or walls, surround the community. And from there, rather than excusing more sprawl with a green patina, developers might even encourage the green redevelopment of portions of strip-mall America into Dutch-style eco-communities, where nature would be an essential strand in the fabric of the urban neighborhood.

In similar ways, the leave-no-child-inside movement could become one of the best ways to challenge other entrenched conceptions—for example, the current, test-centric definition of education reform. Bring unlike-minded people through the doorway to talk about the effect of society's nature-deficit on child development, and pretty soon they'll be asking hard questions: Just why have school districts canceled field trips and recess and environmental education? And why doesn't our school have windows that open and natural light? At a deeper level, when we challenge schools to incorporate place-based learning in the natural world, we will help students realize that school isn't supposed to be a polite form of incarceration, but a portal to the wider world.

All this may be wishful thinking, of course, at least in the short run. But as Martin Luther King Jr. often said, the success of any social movement depends on its ability to show a world where people will want to go. The point is that thinking about children's need for nature helps us begin to paint a picture of that world—which is something that has to be done, because the price of not painting that picture is too high.

Within the space of a few decades, the way children understand and experience their neighborhoods and the natural world has changed radically. Even as children and teenagers become more aware of global threats to the environment, their physical contact, their intimacy with nature, is fading. As one suburban fifth grader put it to me, in what has become the signature epigram of the children-and-nature movement: "I like to play indoors better 'cause that's where all the electrical outlets are."

His desire is not at all uncommon. In a typical week, only 6 percent of children ages nine to thirteen play outside on their own. Studies by the National Sporting Goods Association and by American Sports Data, a research firm, show a dramatic decline in the past decade in such outdoor activities as swimming and fishing. Even bike riding is down 31 percent since 1995. In San Diego, according to a survey by the nonprofit Aquatic Adventures, 90 percent of inner-city kids do not know how to swim; 34 percent have never been to the beach. In suburban Fort Collins, Colorado, teachers shake their heads in dismay when they describe the many students who have never been to the mountains visible year-round on the western horizon.

Urban, suburban, and even rural parents cite a number of everyday reasons why their children spend less time in nature than they themselves did, including disappearing access to natural areas, competition from television and computers, dangerous traffic, more homework, and other pressures. Most of all, parents cite fear of stranger-danger. Conditioned by round-the-clock news coverage, they believe in an epidemic of abductions by strangers, despite evidence that the number of child-snatchings (about a hundred a year) has remained roughly the same for two decades, and that the rates of violent crimes against young people have fallen to well below 1975 levels.

Yes, there are risks outside our homes. But there are also risks in raising children under virtual protective house arrest:

threats to their independent judgment and value of place, to their ability to feel awe and wonder, to their sense of stewardship for the Earth—and, most immediately, threats to their psychological and physical health. The rapid increase in childhood obesity leads many health-care leaders to worry that the current generation of children may be the first since World War II to die at an earlier age than their parents. Getting kids outdoors more, riding bikes, running, swimming—and, especially, experiencing nature directly—could serve as an antidote to much of what ails the young.

The physical benefits are obvious, but other benefits are more subtle and no less important. Take the development of cognitive functioning. Factoring out other variables, studies of students in California and nationwide show that schools that use outdoor classrooms and other forms of experiential education produce significant student gains in social studies, science, language arts, and math. One 2005 study by the California Department of Education found that students in outdoor science programs improved their science testing scores by 27 percent.

And the benefits go beyond test scores. According to a range of studies, children in outdoor-education settings show increases in self-esteem, problem solving, and motivation to learn. "Natural spaces and materials stimulate children's limitless imaginations," says Robin Moore, an international authority on the design of environments for children's play, learning, and education, "and serve as the medium of inventiveness and creativity." Studies of children in schoolyards with both green areas and manufactured play areas have found that children engaged in more creative forms of play in the green areas, and they also played more cooperatively. Recent research also shows a positive correlation between the length of children's attention spans and direct experience in nature. Studies at the University of Illinois show that time in natural settings significantly reduces symptoms of attention-deficit (hyperactivity) disorder in children as young as age five. The research also shows the experience helps reduce negative stress and protects psychological well-being, especially in children undergoing the most stressful life events.

Even without corroborating evidence or institutional help, many parents notice significant changes in their children's stress levels and hyperactivity when they spend time outside. "My son is still on Ritalin, but he's so much calmer in the outdoors that we're seriously considering moving to the mountains," one mother tells me. Could it simply be that he needs more physical activity? "No, he gets that, in sports," she says. Similarly, the back page of an October issue of San Francisco magazine displays a vivid photograph of a small boy, eyes wide with excitement and joy, leaping and running on a great expanse of California beach, storm clouds and towering waves behind him. A short article explains that the boy was hyperactive, he had been kicked out of his school, and his parents had not known what to do with him—but they had observed how nature engaged and soothed him. So for years they took their son to beaches, forests, dunes, and rivers to let nature do its work.

The photograph was taken in 1907. The boy was Ansel Adams.

Last spring, I found myself wandering down a path toward the Milwaukee River, where it runs through the urban Riverside Park. At first glance, there was nothing unusual about the young people I encountered. A group of modern inner-city high school students, they dressed in standard hip-hop fashion. I would have expected to see in their eyes the cynicism so fashionable now, the jaded look of what D. H. Lawrence long ago called the "know-it-all state of mind." But not today. Cast-

ing their fishing lines from the muddy bank of the Milwaukee
River, they were laughing with pleasure. They were totally im-
mersed in the fishing, delighted by the lazy brown river and
the landscape of the surrounding park, designed in the late
nineteenth century by Frederick Law Olmsted, the founder of
American landscape architecture. Ducking a few backcasts,
I walked through the woods to the two-story Urban Ecology
Center, made of lumber recycled from abandoned buildings.

When this Milwaukee park was established it was a tree-
lined valley, with a waterfall, a hill for sledding, and places
for skating and swimming, fishing and boating. But when
adjacent Riverside High School was expanded in the 1970s,
some of the topography was flattened to create sports fields.
Industrial and other pollution made the river unfit for human contact, park maintenance declined, and crime became
a problem. Then, in the early 1990s, something remarkable
happened. A retired biophysicist started a small outdoor-
education program in the abandoned park. A dam on the
river was removed in 1997, and natural water flow flushed
out contaminants. Following a well-established pattern, crime
decreased as more people used the park. Over the years, the
outdoor-education program evolved into the nonprofit Urban
Ecology Center, which annually hosts more than eighteen
thousand student visits from twenty-three schools in the surrounding neighborhoods.

The center's director, Ken Leinbach, a former science
teacher, was giving me a tour. "Many teachers would like to
use outdoor classrooms, but they don't feel they're trained
adequately. When the schools partner with us, they don't have
to worry about training," he said. An added benefit: the center
welcomes kids from the surrounding neighborhood, so they
no longer associate the woods only with danger, but with
joy and exploration as well. Later, we climbed to the top of a

wooden tower, high above the park. Leinbach explained that the tower creates the impression that someone is watching over the kids—literally.

"From up here, I once tracked and gave phone reports to the police about a driver who was trying to hit people on the bike path," he said, looking across the treetops. "Except for that incident, no serious violent crime has occurred in the park in the past five years. We see environmental education as a great tool for urban revitalization." Even as it shows how nature can be better woven into cities, the Urban Ecology Center also helps paint a portrait of an educational future that many of us would like to see: every school connected to an outdoor classroom, as school districts partner with nature centers, nature preserves, ranches, and farms, to create the new schoolyards.

Such a future is embodied in the nature-themed schools that have begun sprouting up nationwide, like the Schlitz Audubon Nature Center Preschool, where, as the *Milwaukee Journal Sentinel* reported in April 2006, "a 3-year-old can identify a cedar tree and a maple—even if she can't tell you what color pants she's wearing. And a 4-year-old can tell the difference between squirrel and rabbit tracks—even if he can't yet read any of the writing on a map. Young children learn through the sounds, scents, and seasons of the outdoors." Taking cues from the preschool's success in engaging children, an increasing number of nature centers are looking to add preschool programs not only to meet the demand for early childhood education but also to "create outdoor enthusiasts at a young age," the *Journal Sentinel* reported. And their success points to a doorway into the larger challenge—to better care for the health of the Earth.

Studies show that almost to a person conservationists or environmentalists—whatever we want to call them—had some transcendent experience in nature when they were children. For some, the epiphanies took place in a national park; for others, in the clump of trees at the end of the cul-de-sac. But if experiences in nature are radically reduced for future generations, where will stewards of the Earth come from? A few months ago, I visited Ukiah, California, a mountain town nestled in the pines and fog. Ukiah is Spotted Owl Central, a town associated with the swirling controversy regarding logging, old growth, and endangered species. This is one of the most bucolic landscapes in our country, but local educators and parents report that Ukiah kids aren't going outside much anymore. So who will care about the spotted owl in ten or fifteen years?

Federal and state conservation agencies are asking such questions with particular urgency. The reason: though the roads at some U.S. national parks remain clogged, overall visits by Americans have dropped by 25 percent since 1987, few people get far from their cars, and camping is on the decline. And such trends may further reduce political support for parks. In October 2006, the superintendent of Yellowstone National Park joined the cadre of activists around the country calling for a no-child-left-inside campaign to make children more comfortable with the outdoors. In a similar move, the U.S. Forest Service is launching More Kids in the Woods, which would fund local e=orts to get children outdoors.

Nonprofit environmental organizations are also showing a growing interest in how children engage with nature. In early 2006, the Sierra Club intensified its commitment to connecting children to nature through its Inner City Outings program for at-risk youths, and it has ramped up its legislative efforts in support of environmental education. The National Wildlife Federation is rolling out the Green Hour, a national campaign to persuade parents to encourage their children to spend one

hour a day in nature. John Flicker, president of the National
Audubon Society, is campaigning for the creation of a family-
focused nature center in every congressional district in the
nation. "Once these centers are embedded, they're almost
impossible to kill," says Flicker. "They help create a political
constituency right now, but also build a future political base
for conservation."

Proponents of a new San Diego Regional Canyonlands
Park, which would protect the city's unique web of urban
canyons, have adjusted their efforts to address these younger
constituents. "In addition to the other arguments to do this,
such as protecting wildlife," says Eric Bowlby, Sierra Club
Canyons Campaign coordinator, "we've been talking about the
health and educational benefits of these canyons to kids. People who may not care about endangered species do care about
their kids' health." For conservationists, it could be a small
step from initiatives like these to the idea of dedicating a por-
tion of any proposed open space to children and families in
the surrounding area. The acreage could include nature centers, which ideally would provide outdoor-oriented preschools
and other offerings. Of course, such programs must teach
children how to step lightly on natural habitats, especially
ones with endangered species. But the outdoor experiences of
children are essential for the survival of conservation. And so
the truth is that the human child in nature may be the most
important indicator species of future sustainability.

The future of children in nature has profound implications not only for the conservation of land but also for the
direction of the environmental movement. If society embraces
something as simple as the health benefits of nature experiences for children, it may begin to re-evaluate the worth of
"the environment." While public-health experts have traditionally associated environmental health with the absence of

toxic pollution, the definition fails to account for an equally valid consideration: how the environment can *improve* human health. Seen through that doorway, nature isn't a problem, it's the solution: environmentalism is essential to our own well-being. Howard Frumkin, director of the National Center for Environmental Health, points out that future research about the positive health effects of nature should be conducted in collaboration with architects, urban planners, park designers, and landscape architects. "Perhaps we will advise patients to take a few days in the country, to spend time gardening," he wrote in a 2001 *American Journal of Preventive Medicine* article, "or [we will] build hospitals in scenic locations, or plant gardens in rehabilitation centers. Perhaps the . . . organizations that pay for health care will come to fund such interventions, especially if they prove to rival pharmaceuticals in cost and efficacy."

Here's one suggestion for how to accelerate that change, starting with children: nationally and internationally, pediatricians and other health professionals could use office posters, pamphlets, and personal persuasion to promote the physical and mental health benefits of nature play. Such publicity would give added muscle to efforts to reduce child obesity. Ideally, health providers would add nature therapy to the traditional approaches to attention-deficit disorders and childhood depression. This effort might be modeled on the national physical-fitness campaign launched by President John F. Kennedy. We could call the campaign "Grow Outside!"

In every arena, from conservation and health to urban design and education, a growing children-and-nature movement will have no shortage of tools to bring about a world in which we leave no child inside—and no shortage of potential far-reaching benefits. Under the right conditions, cultural and political change can occur rapidly. The recycling and antismoking campaigns are our best examples of how social and political pressure can work hand-in-hand to create a societal transformation in just one generation. The children-and-nature movement has perhaps even greater potential—because it touches something even deeper within us, biologically and spiritually.

In January 2005, I attended a meeting of the Quivira Coalition, a New Mexico organization that brings together ranchers and environmentalists to find common ground. The coalition is now working on a plan to promote ranches as the new schoolyards. When my turn came to speak, I told the audience how, when I was a boy, I pulled out all those survey stakes in an attempt to keep the earthmovers at bay. Afterward, a rancher stood up. He was wearing scuffed boots. His aged jeans had never seen acid wash, only dirt and rock. His face was sunburned and creased. His drooping moustache was white, and he wore thick eyeglasses with heavy plastic frames, stained with sweat. "You know that story you told about pulling up stakes?" he said. "I did that when I was a boy, too."

The crowd laughed. I laughed.

And then the man began to cry. Despite his embarrassment, he continued to speak, describing the source of his sudden grief: that he might belong to one of the last generations of Americans to feel that sense of ownership of land and nature. The power of this movement lies in that sense, that special place in our hearts, those woods where the bulldozers cannot reach. Developers and environmentalists, corporate CEOs and college professors, rock stars and ranchers may agree on little else, but they agree on this: no one among us wants to be a member of the last generation to pass on to its children the joy of playing outside in nature.

(2007)

LOWELL MONKE

CHARLOTTE'S WEBPAGE

Why children shouldn't have the world at their fingertips

THOMAS EDISON was a great inventor but a lousy prognosticator. When he proclaimed in 1922 that the motion picture would replace textbooks in schools, he began a long string of spectacularly wrong predictions regarding the capacity of various technologies to revolutionize teaching. To date, none of them—from film to television—has lived up to the hype. Most were quickly relegated to the audiovisual closet. Even the computer, which is now a standard feature of most classrooms, has not been able to show a consistent record of improving education.

"There have been no advances over the past decade that can be confidently attributed to broader access to computers," said Stanford University professor of education Larry Cuban in 2001, summarizing the existing research on educational computing. "The link between test-score improvements and computer availability and use is even more contested." Part of the problem, Cuban pointed out, is that many computers simply go unused in the classroom. But more recent research, including a University of Munich study of 174,000 students in thirty-one countries, indicates that students who frequently use computers perform worse academically than those who use them rarely or not at all.

Whether or not these assessments are the last word, it is clear that the computer has not fulfilled the promises made for it. Promoters of instructional technology have reverted to a much more modest claim—that the computer is just another tool: "it's what you do with it that counts." But this response ignores the ecological impact of technologies. Far from being neutral, they reconstitute all of the relationships in an environment, some for better and some for worse. Installing a computer lab in a school may mean that students have access to information they would never be able to get any other way, but it may also mean that children spend less time engaged in outdoor play, the art supply budget has to be cut, new security measures have to be employed, and Acceptable Use Agreements are needed to inform parents (for the first time in American educational history) that the school is not responsible for the material a child encounters while under its supervision.

The "just-a-tool" argument also ignores the fact that whenever we choose one learning activity over another, we are deciding what kinds of encounters with the world we value for our children, which in turn influences what they grow up to value. Computers tend to promote and support certain kinds of learning experiences, and devalue others. As technology critic Neil Postman has observed, "What we need to consider about computers has nothing to do with its efficiency as a teaching tool. We need to know in what ways it is altering our conception of learning."

If we look through that lens, I think we will see that educational computing is neither a revolution nor a passing fad, but a Faustian bargain. Children gain unprecedented power to control their external world, but at the cost of internal growth. During the two decades that I taught young people with and about digital technology, I came to realize that the power of computers can lead children into deadened, alienated, and manipulative relationships with the world, that children's increasingly pervasive use of computers jeopardizes their ability to belong fully to human and biological communities—ultimately jeopardizing the communities themselves.

Several years ago I participated in a panel discussion on Iowa Public Television that focused on some "best practices" for computers in the classroom. Early in the program, a video showed how a fourth grade class in rural Iowa used computers to produce hypertext book reports on *Charlotte's Web*, E. B. White's classic children's novel. In the video, students proudly demonstrated their work, which included a computer-generated "spider" jumping across the screen and an animated stick-figure boy swinging from a hayloft rope. Toward the end of the video, a student discussed the important lessons he had learned: always be nice to each other and help one another.

There were important lessons for viewers as well. Images of the students talking around computer screens dispelled (appropriately, I think) the notion that computers always isolate users. Moreover, the teacher explained that her students were so enthusiastic about the project that they chose to go to the computer lab rather than outside for recess. While she seemed impressed by this dedication, it underscores the first troubling influence of computers. The medium is so compelling that it lures children away from the kind of activities through which they have always most effectively discovered themselves and their place in the world.

Ironically, students could best learn the lessons implicit in *Charlotte's Web*—the need to negotiate relationships, the importance of all members of a community, even the rats—by engaging in the recess they missed. In a school, recess is not just a break from intellectual demands or a chance to let off steam. It is also a break from a closely supervised social and physical environment. It is when children are most free to negotiate their own relationships, at arm's length from adult authority. Yet across the U.S., these opportunities are disappearing. By the year 2000, according to a 2001 report by University of New Orleans associate professor Judith Kieff, more than 40 percent of the elementary and middle schools in the U.S. had entirely eliminated recess. By contrast, U.S. Department of Education statistics indicate that spending on technology in schools increased by more than 300 percent from 1990 to 2000.

Structured learning certainly has its place. But if it crowds out direct, unmediated engagement with the world, it undercuts a child's education. Children learn the fragility of flowers by touching their petals. They learn to cooperate by organizing their own games. The computer cannot simulate the physical and emotional nuances of resolving a dispute during kickball, or the creativity of inventing new rhymes to the rhythm of jumping rope. These full-bodied, often deeply heartfelt experiences educate not just the intellect but also the soul of the child. When children are free to practice on their own, they can test their inner perceptions against the world around them, develop the qualities of care, self-discipline, courage, compassion, generosity, and tolerance—and gradually figure out how to be part of both social and biological communities.

It's true that engaging with others on the playground can be a harrowing experience, too. Children often need to be monitored and, at times, disciplined for acts of cruelty, carelessness, selfishness, even violence. Computers do provide an attractively reliable alternative to the dangers of unsupervised play. But schools too often use computers or other highly structured activities to prevent these problematic qualities of childhood from surfacing—out of fear or a compulsion to force-feed academics. This effectively denies children the practice and feedback they need to develop the skills and dispositions of a mature person. If children do not dip their toes in the waters of unsupervised social activity, they likely will never be able to swim in the sea of civic responsibility. If they have no opportunities to dig in the soil, discover the spiders, bugs, birds, and plants that populate even the smallest unpaved playgrounds, they will be less likely to explore, appreciate, and protect nature as adults.

Computers not only divert students from recess and other unstructured experiences, but also replace those authentic experiences with virtual ones, creating a separate set of problems. According to surveys by the Kaiser Family Foundation and others, school-age children spend, on average, around five hours a day in front of screens for recreational purposes (for children ages two to seven the average is around three hours). All that screen time is supplemented by the hundreds of impressive computer projects now taking place in schools. Yet these projects—the steady diet of virtual trips to the Antarctic, virtual climbs to the summit of Mount Everest, and trips into cyber-orbit that represent one technological high after another—generate only vicarious thrills. The student doesn't actually soar above the Earth, doesn't trek across icy terrain, doesn't climb a mountain. Increasingly, she isn't even allowed to climb to the top of the jungle gym. And unlike reading, virtual adventures leave almost nothing to, and therefore require almost nothing of, the imagination. In experiencing the virtual world, the student cannot, as philosopher Steve Talbott has put it, "connect to [her] inner essence."

On the contrary, she is exposed to a simulated world that tends to deaden her encounters with the real one. During the decade that I spent teaching a course called Advanced Computer Technology, I repeatedly found that after engaging in internet projects, students came back down to the Earth of their immediate surroundings with boredom and disinterest—and a desire to get back online. This phenomenon was so pronounced that I started kidding my students about being BEJs: Big Event Junkies. Sadly, many readily admitted that, in general, their classes had to be conducted with the multimedia sensationalism of MTV just to keep them engaged. Having watched Discovery Channel and worked with computer simulations that severely compress both time and space, children are typically disappointed when they first approach a pond or stream: the fish aren't jumping, the frogs aren't croaking, the deer aren't drinking, the otters aren't playing, and the raccoons (not to mention bears) aren't fishing. Their electronic experiences have led them to expect to see these things happening—all at once and with no effort on their part. This distortion can also result from a diet of television and movies, but the computer's powerful interactive capabilities greatly accelerate it. And the phenomenon affects more than just experiences with the natural world. It leaves students apathetic and impatient in any number of settings—from class discussions to science experiments. The result is that the child becomes less animated and less capable of appreciating what it means to be alive, what it means to belong in the world as a biological, social being.

So what to make of the *Charlotte's Web* video, in which the students hunch over a ten-by-twelve-inch screen, trying to learn about what it means to be part of a community while the recess clock ticks away? It's probably unfair to blame the teacher, who would have had plenty of reasons to turn to computers. Like thousands of innovative teachers across the U.S., she must try to find alternatives to the mind-numbing routine of lectures, worksheets, and rote memorization that constitutes conventional schooling. Perhaps like many other teachers, she fully acknowledges the negative effects of computer instruction as she works to create something positive. Or her instructional choices may have simply reflected the infatuation that many parents, community leaders, school administrators, and educational scholars have had with technology. Computer-based education clearly energizes many students and it seems to offer children tremendous power. Unfortunately, what it strips away is much less obvious.

When I was growing up in rural Iowa, I certainly lacked for many things. I couldn't tell a bagel from a burrito. But I always and in many ways belonged. For children, belonging is the most important function a community serves. Indeed, that is the message that lies at the heart of *Charlotte's Web*. None of us—whether of barnyard or human society—thrives without a sense of belonging. Communities offer it in many different ways—through stories, through language, through membership in religious, civic, or educational organizations. In my case, belonging hinged most decisively on place. I knew our farm—where the snowdrifts would be the morning after a blizzard, where and when the spring runoff would create a temporary stream through the east pasture. I knew the warmest and coolest spots. I could tell you where I was by the smells alone. Watching a massive thunderstorm build in the west, or discovering a new litter of kittens in the barn, I would be awestruck, mesmerized by mysterious wonders I could not control. One of the few moments I remember from elementary school is watching a huge black-and-yellow garden spider climb out of Lee Anfinson's pant cuff after we came back from a field trip picking wildflowers. It set the whole class in motion with lively conversation and completely flummoxed our crusty old teacher. Somehow that spider spoke to all of us wide-eyed third graders, and we couldn't help but speak back. My experience of these moments, even if often only as a caring observer, somehow solidified my sense of belonging to a world larger than myself—and prepared me, with my parents' guidance, to participate in the larger community, human and otherwise.

Though the work of the students in the video doesn't reflect it, this kind of experience plays a major role in E. B. White's story. *Charlotte's Web* beautifully draws a child's attention to something that is increasingly rare in schools: the wonder of ordinary processes of nature, which grows mainly through direct contact with the real world. As Hannah Arendt and other observers have noted, we can only learn who we are as human beings by encountering what we are not. While it may seem an impossible task to provide all children with access to truly wild territories, even digging in (healthy) soil opens up a micro-universe that is wild, diverse, and "alien." Substituting the excitement of virtual connections for the deep fulfillment of firsthand engagement is like mistaking a map of a country for the land itself, or as biological philosopher Gregory Bateson put it, "eat[ing] the menu instead of your meal." No one prays over a menu. And I've never witnessed a child developing a reverence for nature while using a computer.

There is a profound difference between learning *from* the world and learning *about* it. Any young reader can find a surfeit of information about worms on the internet. But the computer can only teach the student *about* worms, and only through abstract symbols—images and text cast on a two-dimensional screen. Contrast that with the way children come to know worms by hands-on experience—by digging in the soil, watching the worm retreat into its hole, and of course feeling it wiggle in the hand. There is the delight of discovery, the dirt under the fingernails, an initial squeamishness followed by a sense of pride at overcoming it. This is what can infuse knowledge with reverence, taking it beyond simple ingestion and manipulation of symbols. And it is reverence in learning that inspires responsibility to the world, the basis of belonging. So I had to wonder why the teacher from the *Charlotte's Web* video asked children to create animated computer pictures of spiders. Had she considered bringing terrariums into the room so students could watch real spiders fluidly spinning real webs? Sadly, I suspect not.

Rather than attempt to compensate for a growing disconnect from nature, schools seem more and more committed to reinforcing it, a problem that began long before the use of computers. Western pedagogy has always favored abstract knowledge over experiential learning. Even relying on books too much or too early inhibits the ability of children to develop direct relationships with the subjects they are studying. But because of their power, computers drastically exacerbate this tendency, leading us to believe that vivid images, massive amounts of information, and even online conversations with experts provide an adequate substitute for conversing with the things themselves.

As the computer has amplified our youths' ability to virtually "go anywhere, at any time," it has eroded their sense of belonging anywhere, at any time, to anybody, or for any reason. How does a child growing up in Kansas gain a sense of belonging when her school encourages virtual learning about Afghanistan more than firsthand learning about her hometown? How does she relate to the world while spending most of her time engaging with computer-mediated text, images, and sounds that are oddly devoid of place, texture, depth, weight, odor, or taste—empty of life? Can she still cultivate the qualities of responsibility and reverence that are the foundation of belonging to real human or biological communities?

During the years that I worked with young people on internet telecollaboration projects, I was constantly frustrated by individuals and even entire groups of students who would suddenly disappear from cyber-conversations related to the projects. My own students indicated that they understood the departures to be a way of controlling relationships that develop online. If they get too intense, too nasty, too boring, too demanding, just stop communicating and the relationship goes away. When I inquired, the students who used e-mail regularly all admitted they had done this, the majority more than once. This avoidance of potentially difficult interaction also surfaced in a group of students in the "Talented and Gifted" class at my school. They preferred discussing cultural diversity with students on the other side of the world through the internet rather than conversing with the school's own ESL students, many of whom came from the very same parts of the world as the online correspondents. These bright high school students feared the uncertain consequences of engaging the immigrants face-to-face. Would they want to be friends? Would they ask for favors? Would they embarrass them in front of others? Would these beginning English speakers try to engage them in frustrating conversations? Better to stay online, where they could control when and how they related to strange people—without much of the work and uncertainty involved with creating and maintaining a caring relationship with a community.

If computers discourage a sense of belonging and the hard work needed to interact responsibly with others, they replace it with a promise of power. The seduction of the digital world is strong, especially for small children. What sets the computer apart from other devices, such as television, is the element of control. The most subtle, impressive message promoted by the *Charlotte's Web* video was that children could take charge of their own learning. Rather than passively listening to a lecture, they were directly interacting with educational content at their own pace. Children, who have so little control over so many things, often respond enthusiastically to such a gift. They feel the same sense of power and control that any of us feels when we use the computer successfully.

To develop normally, any child needs to learn to exert some control over her environment. But the control computers offer children is deceptive, and ultimately dangerous. In the first place, any control children obtain comes at a price: relinquishing the uniquely imaginative and often irrational thought processes that mark childhood. Keep in mind that a computer always has a hidden pedagogue—the programmer—who designed the software and invisibly controls the options available to students at every step of the way. If they try to think "outside the box," the box either refuses to respond or replies with an error message. The students must first surrender to the computer's hyper-rational form of "thinking" before they are awarded any control at all.

And then what exactly is awarded? Here is one of the most underappreciated hazards of the digital age: the problematic nature of a child's newfound power—and the lack of internal discipline in using it. The child pushes a button and the computer draws an X on the screen. The child didn't draw that X, she essentially "ordered" the computer to do it, and the computer employed an enormous amount of embedded adult skill to complete the task. Most of the time a user forgets this distinction because the machine so quickly and precisely processes commands. But the intensity of the frustration that we experience when the computer suddenly stops following orders (and our tendency to curse at, beg, or sweet talk it) confirms that the subtle difference is not lost on the psyche. This shift toward remote control is akin to taking the child out of the role of actor and turning her into the director. This is a very different way of engaging the world than hitting a ball, building a fort, setting a table, climbing a tree, sorting coins, speaking and listening to another person, acting in a play. In an important sense, the child gains control over a vast array of complex abstract activities by giving up or eroding her capacity to actually do them herself. We bemoan the student who uses a spell-checker instead of learning to spell, or a calculator instead of learning to add. But the sacrifice of internal growth for external power generally operates at a more subtle level, as when a child assembles a PowerPoint slideshow using little if any material that she actually created herself.

Perhaps more importantly, however, this emphasis on external power teaches children a manipulative way of engaging the world. The computer does an unprecedented job of facilitating the manipulation of symbols. Every object within the virtual environment is not only an abstract representation of something tangible, but is also discrete, floating freely in a digital sea, ready at hand for the user to do with as she pleases. A picture of a tree on a computer has no roots in the earth; it is available to be dragged, cropped, shaded, and reshaped. A picture of a face can be distorted, a recording of a musical performance remixed, someone else's text altered and inserted into an essay. The very idea of the dignity of a subject evaporates when everything becomes an object to be taken apart, reassembled, or deleted. Before computers, people could certainly abstract and manipulate symbols of massive objects or living things, from trees to mountainsides, from buildings to troop movements. But in the past, the level of manipulative power found in a computer never rested in the hands of children, and little research has been done to determine its effect on them. Advocates enthuse over the "unlimited" opportunities computers afford the student for imaginative control. And the computer environment attracts children exactly because it strips away the very resistance to their will that so frustrates them in their concrete existence. Yet in the real world, it is precisely an object's resistance to unlimited manipulation that forces a child (or anyone) to acknowledge the physical limitations of the natural world, the limits of one's power over it, and the need to respect the will of others living in it. To develop normally, a child needs to learn that she cannot force the family cat to sit on her lap, make a rosebud bloom, or hurt a friend and expect to just start over again with everything just as it was before. Nevertheless, long before children have learned these lessons in the real world, parents and educators rush to supply them with digital tools. And we are only now getting our first glimpse of the results—even among teenagers, whom we would expect to have more maturity than their grade school counterparts.

On the day my Advanced Computer Technology classroom got wired to the internet, it suddenly struck me that, like other technology teachers testing the early internet waters, I was about to give my high school students more power to do more harm to more people than any teens had ever had in history, and all at a safe distance. They could inflict emotional pain with a few keystrokes and never have to witness the tears shed. They had the skill to destroy hours, even years, of work accomplished by others they didn't know or feel any ill-will toward—just unfortunate, poorly protected network users whose files provided convenient bull's-eyes for youth flexing their newfound technical muscles. Had anyone helped them develop the inner moral and ethical strength needed to say "no" to the flexing of that power?

On the contrary, we hand even our smallest children enormously powerful machines long before they have the moral capacities to use them properly. Then to assure that our children don't slip past the electronic fences we erect around them, we rely on yet other technologies—including internet filters like Net Nanny—or fear of draconian punishments. This is not the way to prepare youth for membership in a democratic society that eschews authoritarian control.

That lesson hit home with particular force when I had to handle a trio of very bright high school students in one of the last computer classes I taught. These otherwise nice young men lobbied me so hard to approve their major project proposal—breaking through the school's network security—that I finally relented to see if they intended to follow through. When I told them it was up to them, they trotted off to the lab without a second thought and went right to work—until I hauled them back and reasserted my authority. Once the external controls were lifted, these teens possessed no internal controls to take over. This is something those who want to "empower" young children by handing them computers have tended to ignore: that internal moral and ethical development must precede the acquisition of power—political, economic, or technical—if it is to be employed responsibly.

Computer science pioneer Joseph Weizenbaum long ago argued that as the machines we put in our citizens' hands become more and more powerful, it is crucial that we increase our efforts to help people recognize and accept the immense responsibility they have to use those machines for the good of humanity. Technology can provide enormous assistance in figuring out *how* to do things, Weizenbaum pointed out, but it turns mute when it comes time to determine *what* we should do. Without any such moral grounding, the dependence on computers encourages a manipulative, "whatever

works" attitude toward others. It also reinforces the exploita-
tive relationship to the environment that has plagued Western
society since Descartes first expressed his desire to "seize
nature by the throat." Even sophisticated "environmental"
simulations, which show how ecosystems respond to changes,
reinforce the mistaken idea that the natural world conforms to
our abstract representations of it, and therefore has no inherent value, only the instrumental value we assign to it through
our symbols. Such reductionism reinforces the kind of faulty
thinking that is destroying the planet: we can dam riparian
systems if models show an "acceptable" level of damage, treat
human beings simply as units of productivity to be discarded
when inconvenient or useless, and reduce all things, even
those living, to mere data. The message of the medium—abstraction, manipulation, control, and power—inevitably influences those who use it.

   None of this happens overnight, of course, or with a single
exposure to a computer. It takes time to shape a worldview.
But that is exactly why it is wrongheaded to push such powerful worldview-shapers on impressionable children, especially
during elementary school years. What happens when we im-
merse our children in virtual environments whose fundamental lesson is not to live fully and responsibly in the world, but
to value the power to manipulate objects and relationships?
How can we then expect our children to draw the line between
the symbols and what they represent? When we remove resistance to a child's will to act, how can we teach that child to deal
maturely with the Earth and its inhabitants?

   Our technological age requires a new definition of maturity:
coming to terms with the proper limits of one's own power in
relation to nature, society, and one's own desires. Developing
those limits may be the most crucial goal of twenty-first-century
education. Given the pervasiveness of digital technology, it is

not necessary or sensible to teach children to reject computers (although I found that students need just one year of high
school to learn enough computer skills to enter the workplace
or college). What is necessary is to confront the challenges the
technology poses with wisdom and great care. A number of
organizations are attempting to do just that. The Alliance for
Childhood, for one, has recently published a set of curriculum
guidelines that promotes an ecological understanding of the
relationship between humans and technology. But that's just a
beginning.

In the preface to his thoughtful book *The Whale and the
Reactor* Langdon Winner writes, "I am convinced that any
philosophy of technology worth its salt must eventually ask,
'How can we limit modern technology to match our best
sense of who we are and the kind of world we would like to
build?'" Unfortunately, our schools too often default to the
inverse of that question: How can we limit human beings to
match the best use of what our technology can do and the
kind of world it will build? As a consequence, our children are
likely to sustain this process of alienation—in which they treat
themselves, other people, and the Earth instrumentally—in
a vain attempt to materially fill up lives crippled by internal
emptiness. We should not be surprised when they "solve" personal and social problems by turning to drugs, guns, hateful
web logs, or other powerful "tools," rather than digging deep
within themselves or searching out others in the community
for strength and support. After all, this is just what we have
taught them to do.

At the heart of a child's relationship with technology is a
paradox—that the more external power children have at their
disposal, the more difficult it will be for them to develop the
inner capacities to use that power wisely. Once educators,
parents, and policymakers understand this phenomenon,

perhaps education will begin to emphasize the development of human beings living in community, and not just technical virtuosity. I am convinced that this will necessarily involve unplugging the learning environment long enough to encourage children to discover who they are and what kind of world they must live in. That, in turn, will allow them to participate more wisely in using external tools to shape, and at times leave unshaped, the world in which we all must live.

(2005)

MEDICINE GRIZZLYBEAR LAKE

AN INDIAN FATHER'S PLEA

DEAR TEACHER,

I would like to introduce you to my son, Wind-Wolf. He was born and raised on the reservation. He has black hair, dark brown eyes, and an olive complexion. And like so many Indian children his age, he is shy and quiet in the classroom. He is five years old, in kindergarten, and I cannot understand why you have already labeled him a "slow learner."

At the age of five, he has already had quite an education compared with his peers in Western society. As his first introduction into this world, he was bonded to his mother and to the Mother Earth in a traditional native childbirth ceremony. And he has been continuously cared for by his mother, father, sisters, cousins, aunts, uncles, grandparents, and extended tribal family since this ceremony.

From his mother's loving arms, WindWolf was placed in a secure and specially designed Indian baby basket. His father and the medicine elders conducted another ceremony to bond him with the essence of his genetic father, the Great Spirit, the Grandfather Sun, and the Grandmother Moon. This was all done in order to introduce him into the natural world, and to protect his soul. It is our people's way of showing the newborn respect, ensuring chat he starts life on the path of spirituality.

The traditional Indian baby basket became his "turtle's shell" and served as the first seat for his classroom. He was strapped in for safety, protected from injury by the willow roots and hazelwood construction. The basket was made by a tribal elder who had gathered her materials with prayer. It is specially designed to provide the child with the knowledge and experience he will need in order to survive in his culture and environment.

Wind-Wolf was strapped in snuggly with a deliberate restriction upon his arms and legs. Although you in Western society may argue that such a method serves to hinder motor-skill development and abstract reasoning, we believe it forces the child to first develop his intuitive faculties, rational intellect, symbolic thinking, and five senses. Wind-Wolf was with his mother constantly, closely bonded, as she carried him on her back or held him in front while breast feeding. She carried him everywhere she went, and every night he slept with both parents. Because of this, Wind-Wolf's educational setting was not only "secure," but also colorful, complicated, and diverse. He has been with his mother at the ocean at daybreak when she made her prayers and gathered fresh seaweed from the rocks, he has sat with his uncles in a rowboat on the river while they fished with gill nets, and he has watched and listened to elders as they told creation stories and animal legends and sang songs around the campfires.

He has attended the sacred White Deerskin Dance of his people and is well acquainted with the cultures and languages of other tribes. He has been with his mother when she gathered herbs for healing and watched his tribal aunts and grandmothers gather and prepare traditional foods such as acorn, smoked salmon, and deer meat. He has played with abalone shells, pine nuts, iris grass string, and leather while watching the women make traditional regalia. He has had many opportunities to watch his father, uncles, and ceremonial leaders use different kinds of colorful feathers and sing different kinds of songs while preparing for the sacred dances and rituals.

As he grew older, Wind-Wolf began to crawl out of the baby basket and explore the world around him. When frightened or sleepy, he could always return to the basket, as a turtle withdraws into its shell. Such an inward journey allows one to reflect in privacy on what he has learned and to carry the new knowledge deeply into the unconscious and the soul. Shapes, sizes, colors, texture, sound, smell, feeling, taste, and the learning process are therefore integrated—the physical and spiritual, matter and energy, conscious and unconscious, individual and social.

Wind-Wolf was with his mother in South Dakota while she danced for seven days straight in the hot sun, in the sacred Sun Dance Ceremony of a distant tribe. He has been doctored in a number of different healing ceremonies by medicine men and women from places ranging from Alaska and Arizona to New York and California. He has been in more than twenty different sacred sweat lodge rituals—used by native tribes to purify mind, body, and soul—since he was three years old, and he has been exposed to many different religions of his racial brothers: Protestant, Catholic, Asian Buddhist, and Tibetan Lamaist.

It takes a long time to absorb and reflect on these kinds of experiences, so maybe that is why you think my Indian child is a slow learner. His aunts and grandmothers taught him to count while they sorted out the materials used to make the abstract designs in native baskets. He learned his basic numbers by helping his father count and sort the rocks to be used in the sweat lodge—seven rocks for a medicine sweat, say, or thirteen for the summer solstice ceremony. And he was taught mathematics by counting the sticks we use in our traditional native hand game. So I realize he may be slow in grasping the methods that you are now using in your class room but I hope you will be patient with him. It takes time to adjust to a new cultural system.

He is not culturally "disadvantaged," he is culturally "different." If you ask him how many months there are in a year, he will probably tell you thirteen. He will respond this way not because he doesn't know how to count properly, but because he has been taught by our traditional people that there are thirteen full moons in a year according to the native tribal calendar and thirteen tail feathers on a perfectly balanced eagle.

But he also knows that some eagles may only have twelve tail feathers, or seven. He knows that the flicker has exactly ten tail feathers; that they are red and black, representing east and west, life and death, and that this bird is a "fire" bird, a power used in native healing. He can count more than forty different kinds of birds, tell you what kind of bird each is and where it lives, the season in which it appears, and how it is used in a sacred ceremony. He may have trouble writing his name on a piece of paper, but he knows how to say it and many other things in several different Indian languages. He is not fluent yet because he is only five years old and required by law to attend your educational system, learn your language, your values, your ways of thinking, and your methods of teaching.

So you see, all of these influences together make him somewhat shy and quiet—and perhaps "slow" according to your standards. But if Wind-Wolf was not prepared for his first tentative foray into your world, neither were you appreciative of his culture. On the first day of class, you had difficulty with his name. You wanted to call him "Wind"—insisting that Wolf somehow must be his middle name. The students in the class laughed at him, causing him embarrassment.

While you are trying to teach him your new methods, he may be looking out the window as if daydreaming. Why? Because he has been taught to watch and study the changes in nature. It is hard for him to switch from the right to the left hemisphere of the brain when he sees the leaves turning bright colors, the geese heading south, and the squirrels scurrying to get ready for winter. In his heart, in his young mind, and almost by instinct, he knows that this is the time of year he is supposed to be with his people gathering and preparing fish, deer meat, and plants and herbs, and learning his tasks in this role. He is caught between two worlds.

Yesterday, for the third time in two weeks, he came home crying and said he wanted to have his hair cut. He said he doesn't have any friends at school because they make fun of his long hair. I tried to explain to him that in our culture, long hair is a sign of masculinity and balance and is a source of power. But he remained adamant in his position.

To make matters worse, he recently encountered his first harsh case of racism. Wind-Wolf had managed to adopt at least one good school friend. On the way home from school one day, he asked his new pal if he wanted to come home to play with him until supper. That was okay with Wind-Wolf's mother, who was walking with them. When they got to the friend's house, the two boys ran inside to ask permission while Wind-Wolf's mother waited. But the other boy's mother lashed out, "It is okay if you have to play with him at school, but we don't allow that kind of people in our house!" When my wife asked why not, the other boy's mother answered, "Because you are Indians and we are white, and I don't want my kids growing up with your kind of people."

So now my young Indian child does not want to go to school anymore (even though his hair is cut). He feels that he does not belong. He is the only Indian child in your class, and instead of being proud of his race, heritage, and culture, he now feels ashamed. When he watches television, he asks why white people hate us so much and always kill our people in the movies and why they take everything from us. He asks why the other kids in school are not taught about the power, beauty, and essence of nature. Now he refuses to sing his native songs, play with his Indian artifacts, learn his language, or participate in his sacred ceremonies. When I ask him to go to an urban pow-wow or help me with a sacred sweat lodge ritual, he says no because "that's weird."

So, dear teacher, I want to introduce you to my son, Wind-Wolf. He stems from a long line of hereditary chiefs, medicine men and women, and ceremonial leaders whose knowledge is still studied and recorded in contemporary books. He has seven different tribal systems flowing through his blood; he is even part white. I want my child to succeed in school and in life. I don't want him to be a dropout or to end up on drugs and alcohol because he is made to feel inferior or because of discrimination. I want him to be proud of his rich culture, and I would like him to succeed in both cultures. But I need your help.

What you say and what you do in the classroom has a significant effect on my child. All I ask is that you work with me to help educate my child in the best way. If you don't have the knowledge and experience to deal with culturally different children, I am willing to help you with the few resources I have or direct you to other resources.

Millions of dollars have been appropriated by Congress each year for "Indian Education." All you have to do is encourage your school to use these resources. My Indian child has a constitutional right to learn and maintain his culture. By the same token I believe that non-Indian children have a constitutional right to learn about native American heritage and culture, because Indians play a significant part in the history of Western society.

My son, Wind-Wolf, is not an empty glass coming into your class to be filled. He is a full basket coming into a different society with something special to share. Please let him share his knowledge, heritage, and culture with you and his peers.

(1995)

DAVID SOBEL

LOOK, DON'T TOUCH

The problem with environmental education

THE KIDS HAVE BEEN UP since seven-thirty playing computer games and watching cartoons. *What a travesty for them to
be inside on such a beautiful day,* you harrumph to yourself. On
the refrigerator, you notice the schedule of events from the
nearby nature center. "Let's Get Face to Face with Flowers," it
beckons. *Just the thing!* It's a sparkly May morning. Buds are
bursting. There's a warm breeze full of the aromatic scent of
the woods just waking up.

You trundle the kids into the minivan. They despondently
consent. "Do we have to do a program? Programs are boring," the older one complains. But as soon as you pull into the
parking lot at Happy Hills Nature Center, their faces brighten.
They fling the sliding door open and scamper down through
the blossom-filled meadow to the shore of the pond. Ross, age
seven, pulls off his sneakers and wades in, bent over searching for frogs. Amanda, age ten, plops down and starts making
a dandelion tiara. *What a good decision,* you think to yourself.

Terri, the smiley naturalist wearing the official Happy
Hills insigniaed staff shirt, saunters over. "Here for the
flower program?" she chirps. "We're meeting up in the Cozy

Corner room to get started."

Ross asks, "Can Freddie come too?" holding up the fat green frog he has befriended.

Terri's bright face darkens a bit. "Sorry. Freddie needs to stay in the pond. Did you know the oils from your hands can make Freddie sick?"

In the darkened Cozy Corner room, Terri has prepared a PowerPoint of all the flowers you might see on the trail today. "Here are some spring beauties. They look just like little peppermint candies. But, of course, we can't eat them. And here's one of my favorites, Dutchman's breeches. Why do you think we call them that?"

After about the seventh slide the kids start to squirm in their seats. "Daddy, I have to go pee," complains Ross. After about the twenty-seventh slide, you too have to go pee.

"And now, let's see how many we can find," Terri says. It's good to be back outside. Upon entering the woods, Amanda notices a red eft in a patch of moss. She takes a few steps off the trail and Terri chastises her: "Remember, Amanda, nature is fragile! When you walk off the trail, you crush all kinds of little creatures you can't see." Farther on Ross scampers up into the inviting branches of a tree that has fallen across the trail. "Sorry, Ross, no climbing, too dangerous, we wouldn't want you to get hurt." At each flower, Terri circles everyone around and tells them the Latin name, the herbal uses, the pollinator, the . . . Once in a while someone gets to touch the petals, only *veeerrry* gently. Picking flowers is strictly verboten.

Toward the end of the walk, the trail comes out by the pond, where Amanda finds her discarded dandelion tiara and slips it into her shirt, watching to make sure Terri doesn't notice. On the ride home, no one talks.

"Well, that was fun," you enthuse, trying to get the conversation going.

Amanda extracts her dandelion tiara and perches it on her head. "Picking flowers was fun. But we told you about programs, Daddy. Too many rules. It would've been fun if we could have just played all together in the meadow." You find that you agree.

Contrast this experience with John Muir's recollection of arriving at his family's first American homestead in remote Fountain Lake, Wisconsin, when he was eleven. Within minutes, he and his brother were up in a tree observing a blue jay's nest. From there they raced about to find a bluebird's nest, then a woodpecker's, and thus "began an acquaintance with the frogs and snakes and turtles in the creeks and springs." The new world of untamed America was thrilling for John and his brother:

> The sudden plash into pure wildness—baptism in Nature's warm heart—how utterly happy it made us! Nature streaming into us, wooingly teaching her wonderful glowing lessons, so unlike the dismal grammar ashes and cinders so long thrashed into us. . . . Young hearts, young leaves, flowers, animals, the winds and the streams and the sparkling lake, all wildly, gladly rejoicing together!

This is the joy of children encountering the natural world on their own terms, and more and more it is becoming a lost idyll, no longer an integral part of growing up. There are many reasons for this loss—urbanization, the changing social structure of families, ticks and mosquito-borne illnesses, the fear of stranger danger. And perhaps even environmental education is one of the causes of children's alienation from nature.

I know that's a puzzling statement. You're thinking: environmental education is supposed to connect children with nature, to get them started on a lifetime of loving and wanting to protect the natural world. Yes—that's what is supposed to happen. But somewhere along the way, much of environmental education lost its magic, its "wildly, gladly rejoicing together." Instead, it's become didactic and staid, restrictive and rule bound. A creeping focus on cognition has replaced the goal of exhilaration that once motivated educators to take children outside.

Much of environmental education today has taken on a museum mentality, where nature is a composed exhibit on the other side of the glass. Children can look at it and study it, but they can't do anything with it. The message is: *Nature is fragile. Look, but don't touch.* Ironically, this "take only photographs, leave only footprints" mindset crops up in the policies and programs of many organizations trying to preserve the natural world and cultivate children's relationships to it.

If you walk the driftwood-cluttered shores along Maine's crenulated coast, you'll find a number of ramshackle constructions in the coves. kid's fort! no adults allowed! a hand-lettered sign will warn. The forts are woven into the spruce blowdown at the edge of the shore, or crouched between the top of the beach cobble and the steep, blackberried bank. Planks, lobster pots, buoys, scrap metal, broken ladders, discarded tarps are pieced together to create bedrooms, lookouts, kitchens, storage cabinets. It is clear that deep, unadulterated play is alive in these salty edges beyond the purview of parents. And yet, on many land trust properties on the coast of Maine, fort building is outlawed because of concerns over liability and unsightliness.

I believe that the imaginative, constructive practice of fort building actually fosters the sense of connectedness that land trusts want to cultivate in young people. It's an instinctive drive to make a home in the world away from the home your parents provided you. When you make a fort, or den, or hideout, it creates a connection to the land, nurturing an affinity for that place. Discouraging these natural tendencies of childhood could actually lead to resentment of, and a lack of commitment to, the land trust's agenda of land preservation. When I wrote an op-ed piece for the *Bangor Daily News* articulating this conviction, one Maine land trust board member responded,

> *Realistically, if the land trust allowed some fort-building along the shore, then how much is too much? Following typical monkey-see monkey-do behavior, if one fort is built, then other people come along and decide to build a second fort, and so it goes. Then we've got a neighborhood of forts that has become a distraction and an eyesore to those who want to teach kids to appreciate nature using a light-handed approach. The scale of fairy house construction on another coastal island is testimony to the scourge this can become.*

See what I mean?

Head south to Texas and you'll encounter more of the same. At the Lady Bird Johnson Wildflower Center in Austin, the trails ramble through hill country chapparal—hardy shrubs, some cactus, copses of woods. It's an unfragile, wonderfully explorable landscape. When I asked if children were allowed to go off the trails, to play in the little pockets of woods, the education director looked at me disapprovingly. "Oh no, we can't let children do that." The intimation was that this was way too dangerous for the children and would have too much impact on the natural resource. I wasn't convinced that either of these concerns was well founded or based on data.

It's true in the inner city as well. When a friend of mine was the education director at the Arnold Arboretum in

Boston, she was trying to create programs that encouraged the multiethnic children who lived in the neighborhood to develop a love for trees. When I asked, "Well, do you let children climb any of the trees?" I got the same disapproving look from her. Tree climbing? Just not possible. Sure, I agree that the rare trees in the arboretum should be off-limits, but the big spreading native maples and beeches, the hemlocks down along the stream—why not? Children have been climbing trees for millennia; it's great exercise, and in the vast majority of cases, they don't get hurt. Keep in mind that children get hurt from falls in the bathtub, and we don't prohibit showers. Similarly, children get injured playing competitive sports. We tolerate the risk of injury from field hockey and soccer because we value the physical and social benefits. Why don't we have the same risk/benefit mindset in relation to climbing trees?

Between the ages of six and twelve, children have an innate desire to explore the woods, build forts, make potions from wild berries, dig to China, and each of these activities is an organic, natural way for them to develop environmental values and behaviors. Instead, the "look but don't touch" approach cuts kids off from nature, teaching them that nature is boring and fraught with danger. Inadvertently, these messages send children back inside to the dynamic interactivity of computer games. Could it be that our fear of litigation and our puritanical concerns for protecting each and every blade of grass are hampering the development of the very stewardship values and behaviors that we environmental educators all say we're trying to foster? I believe so.

As a child in his native Scotland, John Muir vigorously embraced the natural world, having described himself as "a devout martyr of wildness"—a wild child. He was also a courageous inventor.

> *We made guns out of gas-pipe, mounted them on sticks of*
> *any shape, clubbed our pennies together for powder, gleaned*
> *pieces of lead here and there and cut them into slugs, and,*
> *while one aimed, another applied a match to the touch-*
> *hole. With these awful weapons we wandered along the*
> *beach and fired at the gulls and solan-geese as they passed*
> *us. Fortunately we never hurt any of them that we knew of.*
> *We also dug holes in the ground, put in a handful or two*
> *of powder, tamped it well around a fuse made of a wheat-*
> *stalk, and, reaching cautiously forward, touched a match to*
> *the straw. This we called making earthquakes. Oftentimes*
> *we went home with singed hair and faces well peppered*
> *with powder-grains that could not be washed out.*

This is probably not the kind of boy you'd want your children
out roaming the neighborhood with. Dangerous, unman-
nered, destructive perhaps. Certainly, you've never seen an
"Inventing Guns and Shooting Sea Gulls" program on Saturday mornings at the nature center. And yet John Muir helped
create the national park system, and his writing has fostered
environmental values and behaviors in countless millions of
people. My contention is that John Muir's preservationist instincts grew in part out of these childhood experiences, which
probably contributed more to his commitment to the natural
world than learning the difference between sedimentary,
metamorphic, and igneous rocks in the mandated third grade
curriculum.

Or consider how Harvard entomologist and biodiversity
advocate E. O. Wilson describes some of his early formative
experiences in nature:

> *I hunted reptiles: stunned and captured five-lined skinks*
> *with a slingshot, and learned the correct maneuver for*

catching Carolina anole lizards (approach, let them scuttle to the other side of the tree trunk and out of sight, peek to see where they are sitting, then take them by grabbing blind with one hand around the trunk). One late afternoon I brought home a coachwhip snake nearly as long as I was tall and walked into the house with it wrapped around my neck.

Wilson, Muir, Rachel Carson, and Aldo Leopold all had such down-and-dirty experiences in childhood. Wilson didn't just look at butterflies, he collected them. He didn't take only photographs and leave only footprints, he caught ants and put them in jars to observe them. He was a collector, not a photographer, and he was allowed to indulge his curiosity without the scolding finger of an interfering adult. Generalizing from his own biographic experience, he summarizes, "Hands-on experience at the critical time, not systematic knowledge, is what counts in the making of a naturalist. Better to be an untutored savage for a while, not to know the names or anatomical detail. Better to spend long stretches of time just searching and dreaming."

Herein lie my two main points. First, environmental educators need to allow children to be "untutored savages" for a while. Nature programs should invite children to make mud pies, climb trees, catch frogs, paint their faces with charcoal, get their hands dirty and their feet wet. They should be allowed to go off the trail and have fun. Second, environmental educators need to focus way more on hands-on experience with children and way less on systematic knowledge. Or at least understand that systematic knowledge can emerge organically from lots of hands-on experience. Between the ages of six and twelve, learning about nature is less important than simply getting children out into nature.

Terri, the Happy Hills naturalist, could have started the flower program right there in the meadow, having everyone make dandelion chains. (Call it "Removing Invasives" if you must.) She could have chosen three flowers to focus on that morning and challenged the children to learn to identify them blindfolded, by scent only. She might have had the children crawl through the meadow to see flowers at woodchuck level or given them dead bees on probes and challenged them to collect pollen from flowers with different structures. Out of these wild experiences, some systematic knowledge would have emerged. And Amanda and Ross might have said, "Wow, I never knew flowers were so cool!"

Things started out differently for environmental education. The summer camp movement, one of the precursors of nature and environmental education, emerged at the turn of the twentieth century and was founded on the principle of embracing the vigorous outdoors life. One of its proponents, Dr. Eugene Swan, was the founder of Pine Island Camp, a preeminent Maine camp for boys. He wrote, "It will do you more good . . . to sleep under boughs aslant, by a mountain lake with the trout broiling, than to see the Congressional Library or Niagara Falls." And he believed that the "heeding of Nature's ever-calling voice, and an adaptation of our lives to her laws, is going to become a salvation of the American race." Swan advocated for the character-forming benefits of early morning plunges in the lake, living off the land, sleeping under the stars, midnight rituals, and complex fantastical games. He considered his camp to be "the village of Boyville," where campers could be swept up by the "great adventure into the magic land of boyhood." Similar adventures in Girlville soon followed.

He and his camp directors created the War Game, the Whitehead Game, and a raft of other large, complex landscape games that take place over hours or days and challenge boys to run long distances in the woods, creep secretively, detect subtle clues, endure swarms of mosquitos, behave valiantly and heroically. Campers were immersed in, at one with, and consumed by nature. They forded rivers, ate fish they caught and berries they collected, tromped through swamps, climbed trees, constructed forts, followed tracks, captured snakes, did all the things that John Muir, Rachel Carson, Aldo Leopold, and most of the other great naturalists did in their childhoods.

The Boy and Girl Scouts movments emerged not long after. The emphasis here was on primitive living skills—camping in the wilderness, building fires, making bows and arrows, preparing hides, tracking animals. In their original forms, these movements honored the deep inner desire in middle childhood to be self-sufficient, to learn how to survive with nothing but a jackknife and some strands of rawhide. The persistent popularity even today of Jean Craighead George's books—such as *My Side of the Mountain* and *Julie of the Wolves*—suggests that these instincts still persist. The rage over Suzanne Collins's *The Hunger Games* springs forth from this same deep well. These desires are encoded in our genes, compelling children to connect with their wild selves.

From the summer camp and Scouting roots, the environmental education movement emerged in the late '60s and '70s. It started out as nature education, but with all the bad news about rainforest destruction, the ozone hole, and toxics in the environment, it soon became dominated by a desire to recruit children to fix all these problems. The tendency to push things down onto developmentally unsuspecting young children, like the pressure to learn to read in kindergarten, led to the creation of a generation of children fearful of the death of the planet at the hands of uncaring humans. A UNESCO definition from the late '70s says that "environmental education . . . should prepare the individual for life through an understanding of the *major problems* [emphasis mine] of the contemporary world, and the provision of skills and attributes needed to play a productive role towards improving life and protecting the environment."

Meanwhile, in formal educational spheres, environmental education wanted to play with the big boys. It wanted to be more like reading and math and science, wanted to be more incorporated into the academic standards. As a result, environmental education got reduced to a set of facts to be mastered, content to be internalized and regurgitated. In the efforts to gain legitimacy and solve pressing problems, all the joy was sucked out of environmental education.

The big question is: what's the most effective way to parent and educate children so that they will grow up to behave in environmentally responsible ways? Or, more specifically, what kinds of learning, or what kinds of experience, will most likely shape young adults who want to protect the environment, serve on conservation commissions, think about the implications of their consumer decisions, and minimize the environmental footprints of their personal lives and the organizations where they work? Interestingly, there's an emergent body of research that's starting to clarify the relationship between childhood experience and adult stewardship behavior.

First, a number of researchers surveyed environmentalists to determine if there were any similarities in their childhood experiences that might have led to their having strong ecological values or their choice of an environmental career. When Louise Chawla of the University of Colorado reviewed these studies, she found a striking pattern. Most environmentalists attributed their commitment to a combination of two sources, "many hours spent outdoors in a keenly remembered wild or semi-wild place in childhood or adolescence, and an adult who taught respect for nature." Involvement with organizations like Scouts or environmental clubs was cited by significantly fewer of the respondents. Chawla found that environmentalists talk about free play and exploration in nature, and family members who focused their attention on plants or animal behavior. They don't talk much about formal education and informal nature education. Only in late childhood and adolescence do summer camp, teachers, and environmental clubs start to show up as being contributors to the individual's environmental values and behaviors. It seems that allowing children to be "untutored savages" early on can lead to environmental knowledge in due time.

Some researchers then said: Well, let's not only look at environmentalists. How about the general public, Joe the plumber? What affects whether they develop environmental attitudes and behaviors? Nancy Wells and Kristi Lekies from Cornell University took on this question, and described their findings in "Nature and the Life Course: Pathways from Childhood Nature Experiences to Adult Environmentalism." The study is based on interviews with two thousand adults (plumbers, teachers, accountants, nurses, policemen) ranging in age from eighteen to ninety, chosen randomly from more than one hundred urban areas around the country. The researchers compared three kinds of childhood nature experience—wild nature experience, domesticated nature experience, and environmental education. They found that

> *childhood participation in "wild" nature, such as hiking or playing in the woods, camping, and hunting or fishing, as well as participation with "domesticated" nature such as picking flowers or produce, planting trees or seeds, and caring for plants in childhood have a positive relationship*

to adult environmental values. "Wild nature" partici-
pation is also positively associated with environmental
behaviors in adulthood.

Let me translate and elaborate. They found that wild
nature experience in childhood correlates with adult environmental values and behavior. Domesticated nature experience
correlates with adult environmental values but not so much
with behavior. Perhaps most surprising, the study found
that, "participation in environmental education programs (in
school, in Scouts, at camp, or in community environmental
improvement programs) was not a significant predictor of
either environmental attitudes or behaviors."

Uh-oh! The whole environmental education community
kind of flinched when this finding surfaced. But the researchers
were quick to say that their surveys weren't really fine grained
enough to differentiate between environmental education
experiences that were didactic and distancing versus those that
were more hands-on, exploratory, and encouraged that kind of
wild nature play that happens in Boyville. Either way, the take-
away message remains the same: there's something valuable in
letting children wildly, gladly rejoice together. Catching frogs,
making dandelion chains, gamboling through the meadows,
playing Sally the Salamander all play a role in encouraging children to grow up into adults who recycle.

Jim Pease at Iowa State extended the investigation into the
heartland, where he looked at this same relationship between
childhood experiences and adult environmental stewardship
behavior in farmers. He decided that he'd focus his study on
farmers who took advantage of wetlands set-aside funding,
which provides funding to farmers who voluntarily set aside
some of their acreage from crop production and allow it to
be used by migrating waterfowl. Essentially, they're taking a

reduction in income in order to help wildlife. He identified
300 similar Iowa farmers, 150 who took advantage of wetlands
set-aside funding and 150 who didn't. Then he did comprehensive interviews and questionnaires with all of them about
their childhood experiences. He found that the farmers who
displayed stewardship behavior had a statistically higher likeli-
hood to report the following childhood experiences: hunting
and fishing with parents as children, berry picking and mush-
room collecting with parents as children, horseback riding, access to play in natural areas, and reading books about nature.

As was the case with the Wells and Lekies study, wild
nature play, both unstructured or structured by parents but
with the element of unpredictability in hunting and fishing
and riding, were the experiences that seemed to incline the
individual toward adult stewardship. In other words, it looks
like activities that involve taking and eating (as opposed to just
looking and learning), in conjunction with parents who model
thoughtful use, are precursors to environmental behavior.

"For special places to work their magic on kids," wrote lepidop-
terist Robert Michael Pyle, "they need to be able to do some
clamber and damage. They need to be free to climb trees, muck
about, catch things, and get wet—above all, to leave the trail."
Luckily, there are numerous environmental education programs that allow children to play deeply in nature.

One organization that supports children's freedom to
roam, play, even build on preserved land is the Harris Center
for Conservation Education. The Harris Center is a New
Hampshire education center and land trust with one of the
most comprehensive family engagement and education
programs in northern New England. The staff recognizes that
many adults with environmental values speak fondly of childhood experiences like fort building and attribute their land

preservation values to these early experiences. Thus, one of their popular offerings for children is "The Forts, Shelters and Shanties Club." The public announcement reads,

> *Build it, live it and love it! If you love building forts and want to find out how to build different styles of forts, shelters and even shanties, here's your chance. Adventure awaits you in this club, as you create and build a wide range of different styles of outdoor and even a few indoor forts. Also included will be knot tying, fire building and wild tool construction.*

During one afternoon a week for six weeks, children develop those foundational skills that were at the heart of Baden Powell's original conception of Scouting—woodcraft, living off the land, observation. And, from the Harris Center's perspective, they are also, hopefully, becoming future contributors to land preservation initiatives.

Wildly, gladly rejoicing together has taken root in the heartland as well. For a number of years, the Minnetrista gardens and cultural center in Muncie, Indiana, has conducted a Flower Fairies program. For three weeks prior to the Midsummer's Eve, a dancer trains local children to each develop a flower fairy persona. This program started out being for girls, but when boys expressed an interest, they were allowed to participate as well. Each child chooses a flower, learns its attributes, and then develops a movement repertoire based on the flower's attributes. The child and teacher also develop a costume based on the appearance of the flower. For two or three nights around the summer solstice, the center invites the community to come stroll the brick pathways through the preserved Ball Estate Victorian gardens. The candlelit pathways are haunted with glimpses of flower fairies frolicking amid the azaleas, lilies, and periwinkle. A child's intrigue with fairies, and the desire to be a fairy, is used as the bridge to understanding the unique appearance and character of differ-ent flowers. Isn't this a foundational understanding of biodi-versity? Wouldn't you rather do this than sit through Terri's PowerPoint?

For a particularly inspiring look at how things could be different, allow me to take you on a down-and-dirty outing with the Wilderness Youth Project in Santa Barbara, Califor-nia. We assemble at Tucker's Grove County Park, a sliver of creek and forest nestled in between subdivisions. Not really wilderness, but it feels wild enough and far enough away for children to feel immersed. There are about a dozen children aged seven to eleven—black, white, Latino—three leaders, and a handful of parents. The vibe is upbeat and energetic. No PowerPoints here. We circle up in the meadow and get our marching orders: explore our way up the dry streambed till we get to a sheltered pool with great mud for a mud fight.

Not far up the trail, there's a steep bank down to the dry creekbed. A couple of youngsters start to seat-slide down the crumbly bank. It's messy and a bit fast yet there are no admo-nitions to stay on the trail. Rather, one leader goes down to the bottom to catch kids and dust them off, while another stays at the top to manage the flow. A few hundred yards up the trail, we come upon a fallen oak. Kids immediately jump up to balance-beam walk along the trunk and limbs then jump off. It's a little risky. But instead of hustling them along, the lead-ers realize this kind of spontaneous play is exactly what the children need to be doing.

Round the next bend, we come to a fence with a gate. Most everyone goes through the gate, but one of the boys wants to try to climb over the fence, which is topped with a strand of barbed wire. I brace myself for the typical adult

response, "No, José, you might rip your pants," or "Why
don't you just go through the gate?" or "Let me lift you over,"
or "Please stop that! It's too dangerous." Instead, as soon as
Kelly, one of the mentors, recognizes his intention, she says,
"Great idea to try to climb over, José. Would you like me to
spot you?" Once he's over, she crows, "Good job! I knew you
could do it." I'm impressed that his intention is noticed,
validated, and encouraged. Moreover, she refrains from
overinvolvement, providing just enough support to make the
process reasonably safe but letting him solve the problem. A
supportive, can-do attitude prevails, and fear is banished.

When we come upon a child-sized fort, made by a previ-
ous group to simulate a wood rat's nest, the children immediately start to crawl through it. Becka says, "This is so awesome. I am *so* not afraid in here. I could live here and do all
my projects here." As soon as she is out, she says, "I'm going
to do it again," and there was time for that.

A few minutes later some of the boys find a little hole in
the trail and wonder what made it. They probe it with sticks
and then decide to hide some treasures in it, cover it up, and
look for it on the way back. An hour later—though it's hard
to differentiate this stretch of trail from sections that look just
like it, and no adult reminds them to look—they remember
the spot and are thrilled to unearth an acorn, a marble rock, a
sprig of clover. What an appropriate way to develop observation skills—all self-constructed by the children.

One of the kids captures a big, hoppy bug in his hands
and shows it to Mark, one of the mentors. I prepare myself for
the boring mini natural history lecture, "Oh, that's *Idiostatus
aequalis.* We call it a California katydid and it only lives in the
west-facing coastal chaparral slopes. It has six legs and three
body parts—the head, abdomen, and the thorax, and blah,
blah, blah . . ." Instead, Mark says, "Hmm, I wonder what that

is? Hey, how many legs does it have? Wow, look at those big eyes—they look kind of greenish to me. What color do they look like to you? What should we call this bug?" Later on, during a snack break, Mark pulls out an insect guide, finds the right page, and passes it to the children who had been looking at the insect. Instead of saying, "I think it's the California katydid," he says, "Does that bug we found on the trail look like any one of the bugs on this page?" The whole orientation is to encourage the kids to observe, wonder, see patterns, and make sense of things. Names and concepts, environmental knowledge, emerged organically out of these hands-on explorations.

We arrive back at the meadow, wet, mud-smeared, laughing. One of the children says, unprompted, "Three hours isn't enough for these trips. We should do five hours. We should do all day! We should build forts and live out here." It was as if the children had dropped into their wild selves and become creatures of the woods, comfortable and at home in their minds, bodies, and native habitats. It had been just about a mile up and back, but so much had happened. There was never any talk about global warming or endangered species, but there was ample opportunity to become one with the natural world. And all the children were eager to come back and do it again.

This is the kind of environmental education that I believe leads to environmental values and behaviors in adulthood—education that originates in children's innate play tendencies in the natural world; supports and allows wild nature play; recognizes the importance of hunting, gathering, collecting, and, when appropriate, consuming the natural world; encourages adults and children to explore and learn together so adults can model attention and respect; and supports children's appetite for imagination and fantasy. It's environmental education that allows boys to live in Boyville, girls to live in Girlville, and kids to live in Kidville for a while before rushing them out of the woods into Adultville.

As John Burroughs once said, "Knowledge without love will not stick. But if love comes first, knowledge is sure to follow." It's our responsibility as parents and teachers to make sure that love comes first.

(2012)

IN PURSUIT
OF A BIOREGIONAL
CURRICULUM

An interview with John Elder

JOHN ELDER taught English and environmental studies in
Vermont at Middlebury College and the Bread Loaf School of
English for thirty-seven years. He often took his courses into
the field for extended periods of time, substituting the landscape and its lessons for the usual four walls, desk chairs, and
chalkboards. As director of The Orion Society's Stories in the
Land and Watershed Partnerships programs, he served as a
guide and inspiration to many primary and secondary school
teachers who have designed and implemented interdisciplinary
methods of teaching about their local communities—both
human and natural.

ORION AFIELD: *When did you first experiment with teaching
outside the classroom?*

JOHN ELDER: I began to experiment with it about fifteen years
ago, as my teaching at Middlebury College started to emphasize
nature writing and other literature of place. So many of the
writers, from Thoreau up to the present, pursued a journal-

based writing practice founded in observation of nature. So it
seemed that one way to enhance our appreciation of that literature would be to engage in the same kind of activity. Besides,
it's beautiful here in the Green Mountains. It was fun to go into
the woods, take hikes, study the local landscape, and otherwise
spend some time together out of doors.

The first time I attempted something really thorough-
going was eight years ago when I taught a Bread Loaf School of
English course on the Long Trail. Our class was both a writers'
workshop and seminar on northern New England literature. Instead of holding our sessions on campus with occasional excur-
sions, our group of ten graduate students, most of whom were
high school English teachers, started on the Long Trail just
below the Canadian border and hiked south until we got to the
Bread Loaf campus in Ripton, Vermont. During that three-week
period we hiked every day and held discussions and workshops,
both along the trail and at night. Our readings were diverse,
including journals, stories, essays, poems, and Abenaki myths
and lore. We also studied the geology and learned to identify the
characteristic trees and wildflowers of the region.

OA: *What kind of an impact did that experience have on you and
your students?*

JE: I discovered that both the natural environment and our
shared physical experience of it had an enormous influence on
the quality of our community. As we hiked, prepared meals,
set up camp, and helped each other through some challenging
terrain, we also became increasingly attentive to each other's
literary and educational agendas. People grew extraordinarily
alert to both the ideas and the nuances—the wholeness—of our
discussions. I've always believed that a truly successful class
becomes a community—an inspiring, delightful, mutually sup-

portive conversation that transcends its institutional context. Being out of doors together helps a class find its distinctive full- ness in the same way that a tree exposed to plenty of light can express its own inherent form.

I also discovered that a bioregional curriculum works well. My understanding of this term is informed by the writing of Gary Snyder, especially in *The Practice of the Wild*. He con- veys the rewards of emphasizing a particular landscape as one tries to draw connections between human culture and natural history. For us, this meant looking for ways to interweave the indigenous, scientific, and literary lineages of a place, and grounding them all within the shared landscape of our own experience and writing.

OA: *What kinds of changes on an individual and an institutional level will need to happen in order to implement this "bioregional" curriculum, and how might teachers and administrators take the first steps?*

JE: It seems to me that the elementary schools might lead the way. I think that they are in a very good position to do so be- cause they have traditionally been quite closely oriented toward their communities. What they need, to judge by our Watershed Partnerships experience, is a bit more encouragement: to em- phasize interdisciplinary education, to explore the character of their local community—both the human community and the natural community that supports it—and to do more teaching out of doors. I think that programs like The Orion Society's Stories in the Land program, with its supporting publications, visiting writers, fellowships, and summer institutes, will help a lot. When teachers try this approach they find that it's both a lot of fun and really productive for their students.

There are also some specific logistical matters to be dealt

with. Transportation is sometimes an obstacle. To take a group of kids out for a walk in the woods typically involves a bus. In terms of insurance, too, it's become harder in many places for schools to get away with having parent drivers. So I think that schools that want to do this will have to find ways to fund, and to get adequate access to, bussing.

High school and college teachers, with their more specialized and compartmentalized curricula, also have the complication of competing claims on a student's time, and of a teacher's allegiance to a particular discipline. Here, it will be important to come up with models of collaboration, so that teachers can get together and work on a unit that breaks free of the normal sequence of hourly periods where students go from discipline to discipline throughout the day. This involves a lot of planning time, and some grants might really help—giving teams of teachers a chance to work together over the summer. A flexible administration might allow the week to be reconfigured so that several teachers and their students can go off on a trip and perhaps let some other subject matters wait until they get back.

We need, too, to find opportunities to open up the calendar. At Middlebury, it's been easiest for me to teach in an intensive, land-based way either in the summer, when I can take a group of students out for an extended period of time, or over winter term, when in the month of January students have just one course. These are little windows of opportunity, as they say. I believe that more and more teachers may also explore ways to "piggyback" field-based classes on their standard courses at the high school and college levels. When the spring semester is over, for example, they can follow up with a two- or three-week course that takes students off campus.

OA: *Elementary and secondary schools seem to have stronger ties with their communities, while most colleges and universities are so separate from the places where they are located that some even have walls and gates. What might be done to reverse this introverted educational approach?*

JE: I think you describe the pattern fairly. Where colleges are concerned, there's frequently a desire on the part of institutions to emphasize their national status. They don't want to be thought of merely as regional or community institutions, so they often do much less than they could to make a connection with the local environment, lest they lower their status in the academic hierarchy. I hope this doesn't sound too cynical, but that's the picture I see.

Once you've identified the situation, as your question has, you've already taken a big step. There's an immediate possibility for emphasizing connections with other schools in the region, and for a curriculum too that is built upon connections rather than hermetic specialization. One reason for my enthusiasm about environmental studies as an area of inquiry is that it is naturally localized and interdisciplinary. For example, here at Middlebury we have the opportunity to sidestep the abstract departments that have traditionally organized the college curriculum and focus, rather, on a major aspect of our landscape— Lake Champlain. We can investigate not only its hydrology but also its history of settlement, its Native American history, the associated literature, related political and economic problems, the role of the lake in the arts, and so forth. All of these perspectives on the lake are mutually reinforcing. And this kind of integrated approach to place can counteract the specialization and compartmentalization that have begun to squeeze the breath out of the college curriculum.

OA: *Journal keeping is one method that you've used to connect students to their local geographies and communities. Could you give an example of an assignment that you find particularly useful?*

JE: One thing that many teachers do is to ask their students to pick a place, perhaps near their school, and go out and write in that place at various intervals during the class. This is a very common exercise, and yet I think it's a really valuable one too, in that it asks students to look around and figure out a place that appeals to them, to make a personal connection. It also attunes students to the fact that the natural environment is always changing. They see how the time of day or the changing seasons make a big difference to things like quality of light, temperature, the presence or absence of birds, the flowering and fruiting of trees, and the dropping of the leaves. Furthermore, the journal connects the modes of observation and reflection, so just as students observe changes in a locale, they also observe their changing moods, reflections, and memories.

I've also increasingly enjoyed drawing with my students when we're doing a journal-based writing course, and I've been helped a lot in this regard by Clare Walker Leslie. Her approach is that drawing is not, in this context at least, so much about making pictures as it is about seeing.

OA: *How will the idea of place-based education need to be adapted to remain meaningful in our largely mobile and increasingly urban society?*

JE: I do think this is important, because often we talk about the sense of place as if it were related to finding one place and staying there forever. But it's simply the case that most Americans move a number of times during their adult lives. We don't want to make those people feel like failures for not staying in one place. I don't want the people I teach at Middlebury College to feel that suddenly their sense of place ends when they graduate.

We need to do so much more as educators to affirm and support rooted, sustainable communities. But we should also cultivate a perspective of attentiveness to place wherever one is—that lets one be in a new place, too, with a strong sense of appreciation and responsibility for it. A Middlebury student who goes on to live and work in Seattle will experience a dramatic difference between the two regions. But focusing on the specific, local connections of geology, soil, and climate, flora and fauna, indigenous cultures, immigrant cultures, and contemporary literature and art is a habit that can be carried from Vermont to Washington. It is a practice of mindfulness and personal commitment that can enhance a person's relationship to a new home.

OA: *As someone who has nurtured a close relationship with your community and embraced your students as fellow students of the land, what gives you hope for awakening a new awareness of the homegrounds among teachers and students everywhere?*

JE: Hope is certainly the word. I have found these courses to be personally inspiring. Whether I am able to move my class out of doors for just a day or for several weeks at a time, what has struck me has been the sense of enormous energy being liberated. A journal-based practice, connected with nature study and rooted in an intense experience of educational community, is powerful and constructive.

There is such energy inherent in people—expressed not only in the insightful writing and discussion of the high school teachers I encounter at Bread Loaf or the college students I meet at Middlebury, but also in the work that's done by first graders in my town of Bristol and elsewhere. Locally grounded, interdisciplinary teaching can do much to liberate this creativity.

I suppose that my educational philosophy is essentially a romantic pedagogy, as opposed to a deductive or classical approach. I don't think that education, environmental or otherwise, is about teaching people what they need to know by impressing predetermined forms on their minds or filling their vacancy with content. It is, rather, a process of helping people cultivate and extend their inherent perceptiveness. Such an approach is obviously not about creating a single new curriculum so much as it is about a spirit of connection, adventure, and community. This spirit could generate many distinctive curricula that all, nonetheless, accomplish the central purpose of tuning people in to their place and giving them a sense of strength.

(1999)

BELLE BOGGS

THE SCIENCE
OF CITIZENSHIP

What's at stake when schools skimp on science?

ONE OF THE MOST remarkable scenes in Rebecca Skloot's
2010 work of science journalism, *The Immortal Life of Henrietta Lacks*, happens about halfway through the book, in a
smoky Baltimore kitchen. Skloot has been pursuing the reluc-
tant Lacks family for about a year and has finally managed an
introduction to Lawrence Lacks, the oldest son of Henrietta
and Day Lacks. He cooks eggs and pork chops for Skloot and
begins reminiscing about his mother, a strict, pretty woman
who died of cervical cancer when he was a young teenager, but
soon admits that, at sixty-four, he barely remembers her at all.
Instead of memories, photographs, and family anecdotes, he
and his siblings have only the ominous stories of her stolen
cells: that there are enough of them now to "cover the whole
earth," that they have cured diseases, that they will soon make
it possible for humans to live to be eight hundred years old.

After ushering Skloot into the living room with her plate
of food, Lawrence asks her to tell him what his mother's cells
(now known in biomedical research as the "HeLa immortal

cell line") "really did," and Skloot asks him if he knows what a cell is. "Kinda," he tells her. "Not really." Skloot writes:

> I tore a piece of paper from my notebook, drew a big circle with a small black dot inside, and explained what a cell was, then told him some of the things HeLa had done for science, and how far cell culture had come since.

Although their mother's cells—taken without her knowledge during her cancer treatment in 1951—have indeed helped cure diseases and have made millions of dollars for biomedical supply companies, pharmaceutical companies, and research laboratories, the surviving members of the Lacks family still live in poverty, without reliable access to health insurance or proper medical care. Perhaps more significantly, they lack even the basic scientific information that would allow them to understand Henrietta's legacy or make informed decisions about their own health. At Lawrence's house, Skloot meets eighty-four-year-old Day Lacks, Henrietta's husband, who wears flip-flops in cold weather because he has gangrene in his feet; after his wife's death and the re-emergence of her mysterious cells, he is afraid to let doctors treat him. Sonny, one of Henrietta's other sons, refuses angioplasty for the same reason.

Skloot's simple diagram, along with an article she shows him about a method of corneal transplantation developed through the study of his mother's cells, has a profound effect on Lawrence. He is energized by the idea that his mother's cells could help cure blindness, and he convinces other members of his family, including his father, his wife, and his sister, to talk to Skloot.

How is it possible that no one has ever told him how a cell works before? You could speculate that because Lawrence was educated during the time of Jim Crow segregation, he received poor instruction, or that the economic and emotional pressure on his family after the death of Henrietta affected his educational attainment. You could consider the partial deafness, untreated until adulthood, that made it hard for Lawrence and his siblings to understand teachers, or the time Lawrence spent out of school, doing field labor. You could point to his environment, a low-income neighborhood in a poor city, where rumors of body snatching and unauthorized medical experimentation on African Americans engendered suspicion of doctors and scientists. Certainly all of these details contributed to Lawrence's abashed admission that he did not know what a cell was or how it functioned.

But it is also true that the public school system of the United States, the richest country in the world, still struggles to educate our citizens about science and to make that education relevant and present in their daily lives. How well we understand science affects almost every aspect of our personal and civic lives: our health, our reproductive choices, our understanding of the news, how and whether we vote, and our interaction with the environment. Many of the most important and contentious political issues of our time—climate change, hydraulic fracturing, offshore drilling—are also environmental and require an understanding of basic scientific principles that many of our poorest citizens lack. These same citizens will suffer from their lack of understanding: from water quality damaged by fracking, from mountaintop removal, from flooding caused by rising water levels. Poor people are disproportionately susceptible to poor health and more likely to be exposed to environmental or household pollutants. But for many of our poorest citizens, science education is largely ignored, especially in the foundational elementary and middle school years, as we favor the "basics" of reading and math through a testing and school accountability system that does not prepare our students for the significant social and environmental challenges to come.

I was a K–12 educator for ten years, working in rural and urban public elementary, middle, and high schools in California, New York, Washington DC, and North Carolina. No Child Left Behind, signed into law by George W. Bush in 2002, was my constant professional companion, rating the schools where I taught as adequate or inadequate and allocating resources accordingly. This frequently maligned law identified the subjects I taught—English, reading, and writing—as among the most crucial (along with math), and I received additional support so that my students could be successful on the standardized tests that determined my schools' yearly progress. My students received additional tutoring, materials, and time in class, and I was given pedagogical training and assistance from my principals with managing tough classes. Meanwhile, I observed science teachers and classrooms, particularly at the elementary and middle schools, receiving fewer materials and resources, and even less institutional support.

At the elementary school in Brooklyn where I taught first grade, science was a "special," along with dance, art, and physical education. That meant that students were delivered by their homeroom teachers to the science teacher between one and three times a week for less than an hour each time. I remember that the science teacher, a patient but weary man from Jamaica, had little in the room to engage my six-year-olds beyond laminated charts and posters on the wall: no microscopes, no plants, no homemade solar system models or fungus-crowded petri dishes. No fish tanks or worm bins or leaf specimens. Our principal liked a tidy classroom, and his was spotless. She also liked a quiet classroom, and although the kids never seemed especially rowdy to me, he bemoaned their fidgety lack of discipline: in Jamaica, he once told me, it was common for one teacher to control a class of forty or forty-five students.

What did they do in there? Worksheets, mostly, filled with labeled drawings, diagrams, and charts they could not read. Sometimes he performed an experiment, and they watched. Perhaps the best behaved were invited up to help him; most of them never left their seats.

At the time, it did not occur to me to be outraged, or to feel responsible for making up for their lost opportunities. My school was a Title I school; so many of my students qualified for free breakfast and lunch that everyone ate free, and the school day was long and often difficult. I was new to the class-room, my teaching philosophy strongly influenced by Earl Shorris's Clemente Course in the Humanities, a program de-veloped in the 1990s to provide university-level instruction in philosophy, art, logic, and poetry to poor adults in American cities. My students, poor children from Bedford-Stuyvesant, would achieve agency and power in their own, first-grade way: we'd read poetry, study Pablo Picasso and Jacob Lawrence, listen to jazz, write folk tales about our neighborhood.

Sometimes we planted seeds and bulbs in paper cups and left them to sprout on the windowsill, but mostly I didn't worry about science. I was teaching them to read; I was work-ing on their cultural literacy.

But science *is* cultural literacy, a fact that became appar-ent when a friend teaching in the same school told me about getting her fifth graders ready for their statewide science test. Preparation was hurried, last-minute, cursory: their scores would not be held against our Adequate Yearly Progress, after all. My friend, however, did not want her students to feel blindsided by the test, so she had photocopied some handouts and sample questions. "I was trying to explain photosynthe-sis," she said, "and one of my kids asked me, 'How does a plant make their food? Do they use a microwave?' What do you say to that?"

The uncertain student had spent little of his elementary school time outside, had not taken field trips to any science museums. He had not gardened or designed experiments about sunlight and plant growth or even diagrammed a leaf. He had never looked at a plant cell under a microscope. His frame of reference for the world and his relationship to it was severely limited, but teachers and school administrators had worried instead about how well he could read and multiply.

I was reminded of something another friend, teaching first grade nearby, said she told one of her former students, a girl who'd ended the year woefully unprepared for the next year: "Tell your second grade teacher I'm sorry."

We have a lot to be sorry for—and a lot to worry about. Start with climate change, for a particularly fearsome example. Most climate scientists agree that, unless global carbon emissions are curtailed, we are headed for irreversible climate change: an increase of two degrees Celsius by 2040, and four degrees by 2070. A rise of two degrees would likely mean natural, economic, and social disaster—droughts, famines, floods, storms. A rise of four degrees would be catastrophic for human life across the globe.

However, the average American is more skeptical of the seriousness of global warming than he was in 1997.

Forty percent of Americans believe that global warming is not caused by human activity.

Sixteen percent believe global warming is "not that much of a threat" or "not a threat at all."

Certainly the above examples of scientific illiteracy have much to do with our political climate, in which a belief in science is often pitted against a belief in God or the free market. But it is also true that without a proper foundation in science, which ideally begins before kindergarten, individuals are vulnerable to misunderstanding, the same kind that kept Day and Sonny Lacks from seeking treatment for life-threatening medical conditions. They are also easy targets for misinformation and manipulation, the forces behind our country's increasing climate change skepticism.

Recently, the science classroom has re-emerged as a stage for political drama. In his campaign for the 2012 Republican presidential nomination, Texas Governor Rick Perry claimed that his state taught creationism and evolution side by side, because children were "smart enough to figure out which one is right." (Aware that teaching creationism was ruled unconstitutional by the Supreme Court, education officials in Texas scrambled to distance themselves from Perry's claim.) In spring 2012, the Tennessee state legislature passed a bill designed to protect teachers who allow their students to question and criticize "controversial" topics like evolution and climate change.

If American citizens are to have any chance of speaking truth to power, they will need to have a better handle on the truth part. They will need to be better educated, and the science classroom will have to be political—not in the partisan sense, but in the sense of the Greek word *politikos*: of, for, or relating to citizens. The science classroom will need to prepare them for engagement in our democratic society, to make choices that affect their lives and their communities.

So what does an ideal science classroom look like? You might ask Sandra Laursen, codirector of Ethnography and Evaluation at the University of Colorado, Boulder, a research unit devoted to science, technology, engineering, and mathematics (STEM) education. Laursen, a chemist by training, has spent years working as an outreach scientist, providing teacher-training workshops and developing materials with and for K–12 educators. "At all ages, the curriculum is built on well-scaffolded, in-depth, age-appropriate investigations, some of which take place outside," Laursen says. "There is opportunity, increasing with age, for students to branch off to pursue their own interests, but the curriculum and the teacher continually return the intellectual discussion to a few central scientific concepts and the intellectual and social processes of science." Laursen's ideal classroom is equipped with supplies and materials that are maintained and replenished by the school: durable equipment like microscopes and lab glass, but also inexpensive consumables like pH strips, vinegar, toothpicks, and cotton balls. The teacher in Laursen's ideal classroom participates frequently in collaborative, in-depth professional development that is specific to her science curriculum but also places it in the context of science education that takes place in earlier and later grades. (And she is paid for her time.)

This happens commonly at good private schools, which provide their students with highly qualified (though not necessarily certified) teachers; hands-on, inquiry-based learning; and opportunities for educational travel to places like the Galápagos Islands, where they can volunteer to help eradicate invasive plant species, monitor juvenile Galápagos tortoises, and watch the sunset from the pristine beaches of Tortuga Bay. Children from wealthy families are advantaged as science learners almost from birth: they have better nutrition, better health care, parents who take them to parks and museums and who are able to lead them through questions about their environment. They are more comfortable investigating this world, less hesitant about their place within it.

There are public schools, too, that demonstrate quality science learning, though the pressure to perform on state tests often edges out what we know to be the best practices. Perhaps an even greater challenge for many public schools, especially in our poorest communities, is overcoming the deficits of students who don't get a firm grounding in science at home. The Environmental Charter Middle School (ECMS) in Inglewood, California, in its second year when I visited, provides rigorous, environmentally themed college-preparatory instruction to its students, a majority of whom are from minority, low-income families. In ECMS's central courtyard, I heard the constant hum of traffic from the 405 freeway and the low, intermittent roar of planes landing at Los Angeles International Airport. But I also saw abundant evidence of student work and thinking that is tied to experiential science learning: terra-cotta container gardens planted with radishes, tomatoes, and peppers; vermicompost bins made from plastic storage containers; rain barrels catching and filtering runoff from the roof. In the seventh-grade courtyard, students were constructing an aquaponic greenhouse, measuring and cutting the wood framing with the assistance of their teachers.

Getting the students to this level has been hard work. According to Kami Cotler, principal of ECMS, many of her students arrive with what she calls "bathtub deficits. They haven't spent enough time interacting with the physics of their environment." Cotler and her teachers despaired after the school's first big project—building paleolithic shelters after a unit on ancient civilizations—revealed that the students had little understanding of scale or measurement. But after almost two years of hands-on, experiential education, they are starting to improve. "When [the students] were reviewing the aquaponic greenhouse plans, they realized that there was a problem of scale, and they worked to fix it," said Cotler. "That was major."

ECMS has modeled many of its environmental practices after those of its sister school, Environmental Charter High School, which was founded in 2000. In both schools, the students are engaged by the process of learning about science in an environmental context, and they understand how each modification to their campus fits together. The plants are watered with rain collected in barrels and fertilized with worm casings. At the middle school, they eat the peppers and radishes in their salads at lunch; at the high school, they sell plant seedlings at the weekend farmer's market. High school art students paint murals of vulnerable ocean creatures around storm drains, a reminder that even city streets are part of a watershed. Students report becoming environmental advocates at home, encouraging their families to compost or use canvas grocery bags; they understand that there is a direct connection between the things they learn in their biology or chemistry class and the quality of life in their community.

All children deserve an education that allows them to make these kinds of connections, and every community deserves to have its citizens engaged in this way. But too often, when we think about the educational challenges facing poor children and the best way to address them, we focus on the things that are easiest to measure: how well a child reads by third grade, how accurately she solves math problems. In schools with the most at-risk students (and the highest level of testing pressure), science class becomes another opportunity to teach reading fluency or to practice computation. It is cut off from its vital content—*why are we studying this?*—and loses its opportunity to capture students' attention, the way Lawrence Lacks's attention was captured by understanding the impact of his mother's cells.

"Whenever the nation becomes interested, for whatever reason, in alleviating the suffering of the poor, the method is always the same: training," wrote Earl Shorris in 1997. Training, as he pointed out, focuses on the simplest, least cognitively demanding tasks, and prepares the trained for lives and careers that are less remunerative, less satisfying, and less politically influential than the lives and careers of the truly educated. Shorris, who died in 2012, wanted to see the minds of the poor challenged and enriched by the humanities, and he created a rigorous curriculum that exposed poor and uneducated adults to Plato, Aristotle, Kant, and Tolstoy. His primary goal? That students live a reflective, considered life— a life of agency.

Science—the way a cell functions, the vastness of the universe, the effect of development on water quality—can and should have the same impact. But when we replace real, connected science learning with worksheets and test booklets, we are robbing students of the chance to understand what is truly at stake in their lives.

Most recently, I worked at the Hawbridge School, an environmentally focused charter middle and high school in a rural, economically disadvantaged county in North Carolina. Hawbridge's students, who are selected by lottery, come from five different counties to the school, which is housed in a converted textile mill on the banks of the Haw River. Some come for the small class size and individualized attention, others for the program of interdisciplinary study, still others for the promise of canoeing instruction (part of the physical education program) or the chance to grow their own food in school gardens. But not all of Hawbridge's students arrive eager for an ecological or even science-rich education; they come because, like students in charter schools everywhere, they had bad experiences in their assigned public schools: their needs were ignored, they were bullied, or they fell in with the wrong crowd. It is our responsibility, as teachers, to turn them on to the opportunities the school offers—camping, rock-climbing, gardening, monitoring water quality in the Haw River, or listening to presentations by university professors.

Sometimes, like teachers everywhere, we let them down.

Hawbridge students and teachers take a lot of field trips, usually about two a month. Two years ago, during a study of contemporary innovations, we were preparing for a trip to the planetarium. "You know I don't believe in any of that stuff, Ms. Boggs," said one of my students, a junior I'll call Amy.

"What stuff?" I asked.

"You know," she said, looking at the ceiling. "*Outer space.*"

"What do you think is up there then, Amy?"

"God," she said. "And clouds. And Jesus."

Rebecca Skloot might have helpfully drawn Amy a map of the solar system, or taken her stargazing one night, or asked why God, Jesus, stars, and meteorites could not all coexist. I did none of those things, but continued with my English lesson—something about class consciousness and symbolism in *The Great Gatsby*. On breaks, at lunch or before school, I'd been trying to convince Amy to quit smoking, and I was afraid a religious dispute might turn her against me. I didn't want Amy to feel isolated or alienated.

What occurred to me only later is that Amy was already alienated—from science, from ecology—in a way that was similar to Lawrence Lacks's disengagement. Amy had several things in common with Lacks. Her family suffered from a history of health problems. She was fearful and suspicious of new ideas. She worked full time, at a fast-food restaurant, to help support her family. And she was underprepared by the education she received before she came to our school, arriving in ninth grade but reading at a level several grades below.

Luckily, I wasn't Amy's only teacher, and in her senior year she had the guidance of Norma Johnson, who once taught biology at the University of North Carolina at Chapel Hill. In Dr. Johnson's biology class, Amy participated in a range of inquiry-based activities that made scientific principles real to her—reading nutrition labels and tracing her daily food consumption through the metabolic process, examining mosses growing in nearby woods, dissecting a fetal pig, and interacting with guest lecturers from universities and science-based outreach programs. In September and October, Amy used her lunch period and study period to get extra help with the challenging coursework, but she became more confident and independent as the year progressed. She finished the year with a B in biology and graduated from high school with plans to go to the local community college. She hopes to become a nurse.

Amy was one of the lucky ones, entering the school by lottery and finding teachers who not only helped her catch up on skills, but also made the things she was learning relevant to her life. Back at her old school, there are bound to be many Amys who won't be so lucky—who won't get in, or aren't even aware they can apply to a school with smaller class sizes or hands-on learning. Amy's opportunity ought to be everyone's.

Scientific illiteracy is a luxury—one the poorest and most vulnerable among us can ill afford. In an ideal K–12 classroom, every student (and every teacher) would consider himself a scientist, and everyone would be engaged in personally relevant, inquiry-driven science learning. This kind of education, which invites students to observe, hypothesize, debate, experiment, and problem-solve, is not easy to facilitate. It requires content knowledge and experience not only with instructional methodology but also with classroom management. Science teachers in particular need strong management skills and specific and in-depth understanding of their subject matter.

But it's also true that nonscientists can be trained to provide rigorous, exciting, inquiry-driven instruction in elementary school classrooms. "Kids are natural scientists," said Laursen. "They like bugs and dirt, they can observe something for a long time, they're curious. When we fail to capitalize on young children's curiosity and inclination toward social learn-

ing, we turn science into a boring, rote exercise by middle
school, at which point it is often too late to reclaim students'
interest and curiosity." Whatever is outside the classroom
door—a recovering, post-industrial river, a patch of grass, a
cracked cement courtyard—is an opportunity for engagement
with science learning: growing vegetables, designing experiments, observing a colony of ants with a field notebook. And a
community's environmental issues—logging, littering, smog,
development—are also immediately relevant to students' lives.

"I'm not a scientist, man," Florida senator Marco Rubio told
GQ magazine in an interview published in December 2012, following the first presidential debate season in twenty-eight years
to fail to mention climate change. Rubio had been asked how
old he thinks the earth is; it is unclear whether he was signaling
a fashionable disdain for scientific facts or whether he truly did
not know. His full answer suggested that, in his mind, science was far removed from the important work of growing our
economy, and that only people in lab coats have any business
thinking about things like the age of the planet. In his response
to the 2013 State of the Union address, in which President
Obama declared himself willing to take executive action against
climate change, Rubio dismissed such actions as "job-killing"
and suggested that "the government can't control the weather."
Meanwhile, the year 2012 had been the hottest on record
in the contiguous United States, with above-normal tempera-
tures registering every month everywhere except the Pacific
Northwest. That year's drought was the worst in fifty years,
registering as "severe" in more than half the country, and
the record-setting wildfire season, the second worst since the
1960s, claimed an area of land roughly the size of Maryland.
In late October of that year, the East Coast experienced the
second-costliest hurricane on record, an immense storm that

devastated areas rarely hit by Category 3 hurricanes.

After a devastatingly hot summer, and particularly after Hurricane Sandy, Americans began to appear more receptive to scientists' warnings about climate change. Some polls had as many as seven in ten respondents agreeing that climate change is real, and post-election, 60 percent of voters agreed with the statement that "climate change made Hurricane Sandy worse."

On the surface, this looks encouraging. In some respects, Americans may be finally waking up to the reality of a rapidly changing climate. But a response to a dramatic weather event, however convincing, is fragile and perhaps unsustainable. What if next summer is unusually cool, the hurricane season relatively calm? Will we continue to listen to climate reports from NOAA? Perhaps more importantly, there is little indication that respondents to recent polls understand what it would take to turn things around, or how their own actions and choices might play a role. They are not scientists either—not most of them, not yet.

Much recent discussion about the importance of STEM subject education has focused on job training, on preparing our kids and our country to compete in high-stakes and high-income professions. Like Marco Rubio, the majority of students in an average fifth-grade classroom will not become professional scientists or engineers. Every one of them, however, will need to understand skills and ideas connected to the principles of science—what a plant needs to grow, how to read nutrition and medication labels, what it means when their state considers hydraulic fracturing or offshore drilling. Their understanding of these principles will determine how long they live, and how well.

(2013)

ELISE RYMER & ANNE VALLEY-FOX

THE RIO GRANDE REVEALED

An interdisciplinary river curriculum

It begins at the Continental Divide, on the backbone of North America, and its 1,900-mile journey to the Gulf of Mexico makes it second only to the Missouri-Mississippi in length among the continent's rivers. It drains a quarter-million square miles of the Southern Rockies, the Southwest, and Mexico. Yet in certain places and in certain seasons one can walk across its bed and get nothing on his shoes but dust. Of all the world's great rivers only the water of the Ganges is more heavily used to irrigate crops. Yet in 1970 Congress made it the first stream officially named a "Wild River" to preserve its still untouched canyons for those who love the wilderness.

—*Tony Hillerman*

IN HIS ESSAY "Rio Grande," Tony Hillerman describes the vital artery of the land now called New Mexico. Coursing the length of the state, the Rio Grande links communities both literally and metaphorically. It is a lifeline for those of us liv-

ing in this dry land. It has also been described as the most
endangered river on the continent. Knowing how essential
the river is to the people of New Mexico, and knowing, too,
what a threat our habits pose to the river's health, a group of
teachers, writers, and artists came together to develop a river
curriculum for New Mexico middleschool students.

In the spring of 1992, five staff members of Project Crossroads, an education organization dedicated to providing practi-
cal support for teachers, were returning home from a two-day
teachers' conference in Las Cruces, following the river for
most of the way. The station wagon was stuffed with flip charts
and slides, shadow puppets and timelines. We had made
several presentations, attended workshops, and networked
with educators from all over the state. The burning topics that
year included student learning styles, the creation of hands-on,
classroom-ready lessons, interdisciplinary themes, sensitivity
to divergent cultural backgrounds among New Mexico students, and—as ever—how to help students connect with the
taproots of their own knowledge, creativity, and humanity.

An hour, then another, then another rolled by. South of
Albuquerque we passed through Belen, north of Albuquerque
through Bernalillo, and all the while, the Rio Grande bosque
shone brilliantly green in the afternoon light. Talk turned to
the river, and the heated controversy between the city of Albuquerque and the pueblo of Isleta, between urban water use
and traditional use and ceremony.

"Just think of the stories people in these communities have
to tell about the river flowing through their towns and villag-
es," someone mused. She began to describe Jay O'Callahan's
"Village Heroes" tales, with their small towns and seemingly
ordinary people. As we heard of Mr. Payne, the stationer with
the fine watermark stamped on his soul, of Edna, the general
store's clerk who bruised the air with her elbows and had the

heart of a poet, of the village fool who loved all his plants—
weeds included—and wanted every one not to succeed but to
blossom, the communities along the Rio Grande began to link
up and shine in our minds like beads of dew strung along a
spider's web. It was this discussion and ensuing vision that
gave birth to the idea of creating a river study that could speak
to New Mexico students in many voices and forms.

The resulting River Curriculum is interdisciplinary, using
the Rio Grande to involve students in studies of geology, geography, water science, water issues, New Mexico history and
cultures, community civics, and the arts. Through projects
within the classroom and in the field, students are encouraged to discover their place in their community and the river's
place as a source of life, economic benefit, history, and story.

Twenty-five hundred years ago, the Greek philosopher Hera-
clitus posed the question: Can you step in the same river
twice? In communities all along the Rio Grande and its tributaries, we ask students: Is it the same river when it courses
in rapids through the immense gorge north of Taos as it is
when its waters, brown and turbid, move slowly through Las
Cruces? Is the river water sampled and analyzed for organisms, sediment. chemical content, purity, or pollution from
the same river captured on film with cottonwoods lining its
banks and branches hanging over? Is the river over which rafters and farmers contend, industrial users and conservationists
battle in court, Native American, Hispanic, and Anglo users
lock horns the same river to one and all?

As students study in their classrooms, plant trees along
river banks, or tour a sewage plant, they become familiar with
the multiple natures of the river, its almost infinite uses, its
finite acre-feet of water, and its limited capacity to renew itself
once fouled. They learn to analyze data, create watershed

plans, identify with various river users, and try to resolve or negotiate among competing claims. They learn something about public policy-making, channels for citizen action, science-based interpretations of water cycles, the geology of river-making and land-shaping, the art and stories of local peoples, and the influence of the river on our daily lives.

Community members with unique personal experience and professional expertise are invited to share their stories with students and teachers using the River Curriculum: the owner of a sand and gravel company defends his use of river water in his "on-site" interview with an eighth grade class; a San Juan pueblo teacher speaks of the river as a place of ceremony; river rafters discuss the connections between recreation, commerce, and spirituality; a "one-woman farmer" describes how her father taught her the workings of the acequia system, how she now experiments with a dozen varieties of peppers and eggplants, how the sorting and packing seem endless on market days but the reward comes when she's sold out by 7:30 a.m. Through these visits, the workings of the "adult-world-out-there" become less blurred and irrelevant as students catch glimmerings of future roles they might play in the community.

As students listen to the river from its banks, bridges, and dams, as they read what others have heard and remembered and recorded about the river, they are inspired to express their own feelings and thoughts about it. As they begin to personalize their relationship to the river, they come to see more clearly their own dependence upon it.

The current form of the River Curriculum is three loose-leaf notebooks, focusing on science, social studies, and the arts and humanities. Although each notebook can stand alone, and sections can be excerpted from each, the three together create a coherent whole ready for use by teams of teachers who wish to emphasize an interdisciplinary approach to local education.

The *Social Studies Notebook* contains lessons and activities on the geography of the Rio Grande, water law and water usage, and individual and community influence on and responsibility for the river. For centuries Native American communities depended upon the river and its bosque for farming, fishing, and religious ritual Spanish settlers based their agrarian economy on the Rio Grande and its tributaries, and the acequia system became a focal point of social, political, and economic life. The arrival of the Americans brought a surge in economic growth and urban expansion, especially following World War II. Growth created new interest groups whose needs placed an ever-increasing burden on the river. But behind the human tableau remains the river itself, now in danger. Its waters are being polluted, depleted, stored, diverted, marketed. Its bosques are failing to regenerate and wildlife habitats are being destroyed.

In September 1991, Senator Pete Dominici (R., NM) formed a Rio Grande Bosque Conservation Committee to solicit public input on the current condition and uses of the bosque, to identify key issues affecting its health, and to make recommendations about how it should be managed. Realizing that the Bosque Committee provided a real and contemporary model for replication and enactment in New Mexico classrooms, we developed an extended role-play for the social studies unit, based on the Bosque Committee's hearings in Rio Grande communities. Students assume the roles of policy makers, interest groups, and river users: Native Americans in riverside communities, Hispanic farmers, commercial agriculturists, municipal officials, industrialists, recreationists, real-estate developers, scientists, fisheries and wildlife preservationists, public agency staff, law enforcement officials, and environmentalists. They learn the geography and political and cultural history of New Mexico, work in groups to conduct research, gather information through interviews, develop policies, write position papers, and prepare arguments. After enacting their roles before the "Bosque Committee," students are asked to compromise and make public-policy decisions for the overall common good of the community.

The spirit and content of the *Science Notebook* are best described by the kinds of activities it contains: students interviewing municipal water department officials about sewage treatment, water sources, problems and controversies facing the community, and pollution from Los Alamos laboratories; students observing their own and their families' water use at home; classes constructing models of wetlands and watersheds (using carpet scraps, clay, water, plants, and sand); classroom walls covered with huge river drawings from the game "Ecosystem on a Wall," to which students add their own small drawings until a mural of a river and its riparian area is finished to the class's satisfaction. And of course, field trips: students clustered on the dam at Cochiti pueblo, listening to stories about the dam's destructive impact on the pueblo's farmland; younger students acting as tour guides for middle-school students at their elementary school's wet lands; students exploring the Bosque Nature Center in Albuquerque; and students gathered around a sewage treatment pool, holding their noses and making one off-color comment after another.

A journal, kept throughout the days, trips, and experiments of the science curriculum, gives students a chance to reflect on the relationship they're building with the river. When an imaginative teacher can spark their minds with new ideas and broad definitions of what constitutes journal content—field notes, personal reflections, even drawings and sketches—visible examples of learning without subject boundaries emerge.

Journaling is also a key component of the *Arts and Humanities Notebook*, along with the study of literature reflecting the history and cultures of the Rio Grande, oral histories of community relationships with the river, and a variety of arts activities involving shadow puppets, journal- and mural-making, solar graphics, and marbleized paper, to mention a few. It is divided into four sections. "This Is My River" evokes expressions of the learner's personal experience of the river. "Exploring the River" is a creative investigation of the physical characteristics of the river and its inhabitants. "River Stories" brings the community into the classroom and vice versa through reading stories, viewing videotaped oral history interviews, and having the students collect and reproduce stories for themselves, their families, and classmates. The fourth and final section, "Where the River Takes Us," looks at the river through a visionary lens—what do we want for our river? What can we create out of our knowledge, experience, and concern for the river?

Containing over forty activities and including examples from other students' original work, the arts and humanities notebook was created as an expressive and experiential way of getting to know the Rio Grande river system, inspiring students to voice, visualize, and dramatize their knowledge and experience in creative ways. It offers opportunities for personal expression while building skills and self-confidence in writing and other art forms. It provides suggestions for experiences of quiet, contemplative learning, for absorbing information about the river system and the interdependency of various life forms and river communities, and for field trips and projects that bridge the classroom, the community, and the river itself.

Where does the river take us from here? For the Project Crossroads staff and the teachers and students who use it, the River Curriculum continues its evolution; like the river itself, we see it as a work in progress. Since its introduction to teachers in 1993 and during the first of our three summer training institutes for teachers, the curriculum changed its shape as teachers and students helped us edit and revise, deleting some activities and adding others. We have offered workshops for individuals and teams of teachers from fourth to tenth grade levels, provided mini-grants to teachers for implementing the curriculum, established a network of teachers who have taken part in our workshops and institutes, created a newsletter for the exchange of ideas, and held reunions for sharing experiences, new lessons and activities, and suggestions for improving the River Curriculum.

We have a dream: that through institutes and workshops in different parts of the country, the River Curriculum may inspire similar projects in other watersheds, perhaps the Brandywine in Delaware, or the Connecticut River in central Massachusetts, or the Tennessee flowing through the heart of Chattanooga.

In developing the River Curriculum, we have been deeply touched and changed by the Rio Grande. We hear its stories in innumerable forms—rock, soil, landforms, plant life, fauna, geological and contemporary time, myth and scientific analysis, oral history and visual arts, performance and political action, poetry and folktales.

As metaphor and reality, the river sweeps up our passions and concerns and propels them inexorably onward. It is our hope that some similar spirit is evoked as teachers and students deepen their own understanding of the Rio Grande as a collective lifeline and a living presence.

(1997)

ROBERT MICHAEL PYLE

NAMING NAMES

STUFFED INTO the uttermost bowel of a 757, at the ragged
end of a red-eye from Portland to Baltimore, I am consoled
by visions of the Siskiyous. Hours earlier, my wife Thea and
I had returned from those serpentine-girded mountains
in southwestern Oregon. We'd long desired to hike, botan-
ize, and butterfly in that wild country, and now its delights
bloom anew in my mind's eye, coaxed forth by a gentle litany
of names:

> *Kalmiopsis. Azalea. Ceanothus. Brodeaia. Wavy soap
> plant.* Sedum laxum. *Gorgon copper. Leanira check-
> erspot. Babyfoot Lake. Eight Dollar Mountain.* Papilio
> indra: Fontinalis. *Golden chinquapin.*

Lost among the sensations fetched back by these names,
I think back also to a question put by a student in a recent
writing workshop in the North Cascades. "Don't names just
get in the way?" she asked. "It seems that by classifying plants
and animals we just objectify them. Shouldn't their beauty be
enough?" I have heard many versions of this resistance to the
practice of naming names. I first encountered such an atti-

tude when I was in college, in the midst of an excited learning frenzy, gleaning the names of everything I could. Returning to Colorado on a spring break, I found that one of my best friends, who was just discovering hiking and nature, thought that naming detracted from the root enjoyment of flowers and creatures.

While for some this is doubtless an earnest truth, I believe that for others it represents a rationalization. From many conversations, I have discovered three common reasons for avoiding Adam's task: First, many observers are simply intimidated by the sheer number of things with names out there. They feel they can't possibly catch up, so why try? Second, some people are embarrassed that they know so few organisms by name—though this isn't surprising, since it has been generations now since nature study was considered a standard part of primary education. Third, a lot of would-be naturalists are just lazy. As an essentially lazy person, I feel a certain kinship with these last folks. They know it will take some work and application to learn some species by name and cop out instead with the impressionist's excuse.

But there are at least as many good reasons *not* to shun the names of the elements of life. For one, by knowing the identities of other living things around you, you come to understand their relationships much better. This allows you to appreciate your own evolutionary heritage, and how each organism fits into the lineage. For another, these are times when the need for understanding, documenting, and monitoring biological diversity has never been greater. We can all take part in this. But there is simply no way to account for life on earth without learning to recognize the constituent parts and applying names to them. Just as surely, observant and curious people find their pleasures afield vastly enhanced by intimate acquaintance with more and more species. Just watch how birders, butterfliers, wildflower watchers, and other seekers ramp up their enjoyment out of doors by making, and naming, new friends wherever they go.

None of this is to discredit those who truly wish to take nature at face value; nameless does not mean faceless, and keen pleasure and communion are possible without knowing the nomenclature. After all, there is no good field guide to Siskiyou plants, and Thea and I did not feel like carrying two or three large floras and spending our precious time keying. So for many plants, we went generic: that frilly campion reminiscent of the English ragged robin, those elegant little two-toned violets. But at least we often knew the families, could place their relations. And that would be a worthwhile objective for many of us, and a reasonable one. You may not know a cardinal from a pyrrholoxia or a blue jay from a scrub, but with a little watchful time in the open spent with your Roger Tory Peterson, you can easily come to know that this bird is a tanager, that a flycatcher, and the other a finch.

We are landing in Baltimore. When I get to The Orion Society's Fire & Grit conference, all the humans will have nametags on. The other species will not, but that's what field guides are for. As soon as I hit the ground, I plan to scan the trees (sassafras, sycamore, shagbark), looking and listening for warblers (Blackburnian, parula, prothonotary). Along with the Carolina wrens and the great spangled fritillaries, they will be my neighbors for a few days.

And that's what it comes down to in the end: knowing your fellows in the neighborhood of living things. You can smile politely and fake it when you don't know the folks next door or down the block. But when you call them by name, recognition and relationship become possible. As the writer Ann Zwinger perfectly put it, entering new territory is "like walking into a big party where at least I know a few families, and recognize some friends." Those who take the trouble to identify plants and animals, she rightly says, are "at home in a natural world that will offer them challenge and pleasure the rest of their lives."

(1999)

CONTRIBUTORS

Belle Boggs is the author of *Mattaponi Queen*, a collection of linked stories, and *The Ugly Bear List* (forthcoming from Graywolf Press), a novel. Boggs was a New York City Teaching Fellow and has worked in public schools in Brooklyn, Washington DC, and North Carolina. She has received fellowships to the Bread Loaf and Sewanee writers' conferences, the North Carolina Arts Council, and the National Endowment for the Arts. In addition to *Orion*, her work has appeared in *The Paris Review, Harper's, Glimmer Train*, the *Oxford American, Slate, The Sun*, and other publications.

John Elder taught English and environmental studies at Middlebury College and the Bread Loaf School of English for thirty-seven years, where he developed a special interest in environmental education and service-learning courses that introduced his students to the rural communities of Addison County, Vermont. His recent books, *Reading the Mountains of Home, The Frog Run*, and *Pilgrimage to Vallombrosa*, all combine discussion of literature and descriptions of the Vermont landscape with personal narratives. He has recently completed a memoir called *Picking up the Flute*.

Medicine Grizzlybear Lake, also known as Bobby Lake-Thom, is a traditional native healer from northwestern California. He is the author of *Native Healer, Spirits of the Earth*, and *Call of the Great Spirit*. He was a professor of Native American studies for over twenty years, teaching at Humboldt State University, Gonzaga University, and Eastern Montana College. He has served as a consultant for Indian reservation programs, tribes, organizations, and federal and state agencies for over twenty-five years in the areas of Indian health, education, social services, natural resources, religion, BIA 638 programs and contracts, and related grant writing and development.

Richard Louv is the author of *Last Child in the Woods: Saving Our Children from Nature-Deficit Disorder* and *The Nature Principle*. Translated into twelve languages, published in seventeen countries, his books coined the phrase "nature-deficit disorder" and helped launch an international movement to connect children and their families to nature. In 2008, he was awarded the Audubon Medal. He has given keynote addresses at the national conference of the American Academy of Pediatrics and at the first White House Summit on Environmental Education. He is also Chairman Emeritus of the Children & Nature Network.

Lowell Monke is professor of education at Wittenberg University, where he teaches courses on the philosophy of education and the impact of media on young people. He is coauthor of *Breaking Down the Digital Walls: Learning to Teach in a Post-Modem World*, which critically examines his pioneering work with R. W. Burniske coordinating telecollaborative projects for high school students. He recently moved to Bear Mountain in Colorado where he is trying to stay inside long enough to complete a book that outlines a radically different educational environment designed to support a desperately needed post-technological age.

Brenda Peterson is the author of seventeen books, including a *New York Times* Notable Book of the Year, *Duck and Cover*. Her recent memoir, *I Want to Be Left Behind: Finding Rapture Here on Earth* was chosen as a Top Ten Best Non-Fiction Book of the Year by the *Christian Science Monitor*. Her children's book, *Leopard and Silkie: One Boy's Quest to Save Seal Pups* was awarded an "Outstanding Science Book of 2013" by the National Science Teachers' Association. Her new young-adult novel is *The Drowning World*.

Robert Michael Pyle has lived in the Lower Columbia River estuary for thirty-five years. His many books include *Wintergreen* and *Sky Time in Gray's River*, the road-trip epics *Chasing Monarchs* and *Mariposa Road*, and several standard butterfly works. A Guggenheim Fellow and John Burroughs Medalist, Pyle founded the Xerces Society for Invertebrate Conservation. His most recent book, *The Tangled Bank*, collects ten years of columns published under that title in *Orion* and *Orion Afield*, including the essay in this book. His collection of poems, *Evolution of the Genus Iris*, is forthcoming from Lost Horse Press.

Erik Reece is the author of *An American Gospel: On Family, History, and the Kingdom of God* and *Lost Mountain: A Year in the Vanishing Wilderness*, which won the John B. Oakes Award for Environmental Writing and the Sierra Club's David R. Brower Award. He is a contributing editor to *Orion* and is working on a book about the utopian movement in the U.S. He lives in Nonesuch, Kentucky, and teaches writing at the University of Kentucky. His most recent book, *The Embattled Wilderness* (written with Jim Krupa), is an argument to save one eastern Kentucky forest from the ravages of mountaintop removal strip mining.

Elise Rymer has published in *Orion Afield* and *Peregrine* magazine. In 1982 she founded Project Crossroads, a small nonprofit educational resource group in Santa Fe, New Mexico. Through this group she worked in the Santa Fe public schools and several Native American schools until 2005, when she

moved back to western Massachusetts. She has worked with
K–12 students in writing, stories, ecology, and social responsibility since the 1980s. Over the past thirty years she has been
collaborating with storyteller Jay O'Callahan in the development of his stories.

David Sobel is a senior faculty member in the education
department at Antioch University New England in Keene,
New Hampshire. He consults and speaks widely on child
development and place-based education for schools, environmental organizations, and the National Park Service. He has
authored seven books and more than sixty articles on children
and nature for educators, parents, environmentalists, and
school administrators, and his most recent books are *Wild
Play: Parenting Adventures in the Great Outdoors* and *Place- and
Community-Based Education in Schools*. He was recognized as
one of the Daring Dozen educational leaders in the United
States in 2007 by *Edutopia* magazine. David works and plays
in the Monadnock region of southwestern New Hampshire.

Stephen L. Talbott is a senior researcher at The Nature Insti-
tute in Ghent, New York. He is author of *Devices of the Soul:
Battling for Our Selves in an Age of Machines* and also is responsible for the online project "Toward a Biology Worthy of Life."

Ann Valley-Fox worked with Elise Rymer and Project Crossroads staff for twenty-five years. She is the author of four col-
lections of poems, including *How Shadows Are Bundled*, and
coauthored the book *Your Mythic Journey* with Sam Keen.
She also coedited, with Ann Lacy, five volumes of Works
Progress Administration documents from the New Mexico
state archives. These volumes, published between 2008 and
2013 and sponsored by Project Crossroads, can be found

ABOUT ORION MAGAZINE

SINCE 1982, *Orion* has been a meeting place for people who seek a conversation about nature and culture that is rooted in beauty, imagination, and hope. Through the written word, the visual arts, and the ideas of our culture's most imaginative thinkers, *Orion* seeks to craft a vision for a better future for both people and planet.

Reader-supported and totally advertising-free, *Orion* blends scientific thinking with the arts, and the intellectual with the emotional. *Orion* has a long history of publishing the work of established writers from Wendell Berry, Terry Tempest Williams, and Barry Lopez to Rebecca Solnit, Luis Alberto Urrea, and Sandra Steingraber.

Orion is also grounded in the visual arts, publishing picture essays and art portfolios that challenge the traditional definition of "environment" and invite readers to think deeply about their place in the natural world. *Orion*'s website, www.orionmagazine.org, features multimedia web extras including slide shows and author interviews, as well as opportunities for readers to discuss *Orion* articles.

Orion is published bimonthly by The Orion Society, a nonprofit 501(c)3 organization, and is available in both print and digital editions.

Subscribe

Orion publishes six beautiful, inspiring issues per year. To get a free trial issue, purchase a subscription, or order a gift subscription, please visit www.orionmagazine.org/subscribe or call 888/254-3713.

Support

Orion depends entirely on the generous support of readers and foundations to publish the magazine and books like this one. To support *Orion*, please visit www.orionmagazine.org/donate, or send a contribution directly to *Orion* at 187 Main Street, Great Barrington, MA, 01230.

To discuss making a gift of stock or securities, or for information about how to include *Orion* in your estate plans, please call us at 888/909-6568, or send an e-mail to development@orionmagazine.org.

Shop

Head to the *Orion* website, www.orionmagazine.org, to purchase *Orion* books, organic cotton t-shirts, and other merchandise featuring the distinctive *Orion* logo. Back issues from the past thirty years are also available.

MORE BOOKS FROM ORION

ORION READERS

Orion Readers collect landmark *Orion* essays into short thematic volumes:

Change Everything Now. A selection of essays about ecological urgency.

Thirty-Year Plan: Thirty Writers on What We Need to Build a Better Future. An eloquent statement on the future of humanity.

Wonder and Other Survival Skills. A collection of thoughtful and inspirational writing on our relationship to the natural world.

Beyond Ecophobia: Reclaiming the Heart in Nature Education, by David Sobel. An expanded version of one of *Orion*'s most popular articles that speaks to those interested in nurturing in children the ability to understand and care deeply for nature from an early age.

Into the Field: A Guide to Locally Focused Learning, by Claire Walker Leslie, John Tallmadge, and Tom Wessels, with an introduction by Ann Zwinger. Curriculum ideas for teachers interested in taking their students out of doors.

Place-Based Education: Connecting Classrooms & Communities, by David Sobel. A guide for using the local community and environment as the starting place for curriculum learning, strengthening community bonds, appreciation for the natural world, and a commitment to citizen engagement.

ORION ANTHOLOGIES

Finding Home: Writing on Nature and Culture from Orion *Magazine,* edited by Peter Sauer. An anthology of the best writing from *Orion* published from 1982 to 1992.

The Future of Nature: Writing on a Human Ecology from Orion *Magazine,* selected and introduced by Barry Lopez. An anthology of the best writing from *Orion* published from 1992 to 2007.

FOR EDUCATORS

Ideal for reading groups and academic course adoption, many *Orion* books are accompanied by a downloadable teacher's guide consisting of key discussion questions. Teacher's guides can be found on the *Orion* website at www.orionmagazine .org/education.

Series design by Hans Teensma,
principal of the design studio Impress
(www.impressinc.com), which has
designed *Orion* since 1998.
The typeface is Scala, designed by Dutch
typographer Martin Majoor in 1990.
Printed by BookMobile.